MW00614513

VERMONT'S EBENEZER ALLEN

Patriot, Commando and Emancipator

GLENN FAY JR.

Foreword by Former Governor James Douglas

THE
History
PRESS

Published by The History Press
Charleston, SC
www.historypress.com

Cover illustration: An Ebenezer Allen mural painted by Stephen Belaski of Bellows Falls, Vermont. *Photograph courtesy of Ruxana's Home Interiors and the Works Progress Administration.*

First published 2021

ISBN 9781540247636

Library of Congress Control Number: 2021931128

This book is dedicated to Donna.

CONTENTS

CONTENTS

CHRONOLOGY OF EBENEZER ALLEN

1743   Allen is born in Northampton and christened by Reverend Jonathan Edwards.

1755   Allen's father, Samuel Allen, dies at the age of forty-nine.

1762   Allen marries Lydia Richards from New Marlboro, Massachusetts.

1763   Abiel Allen, Lydia and Ebenezer's first child, is born in New Marlboro.

1765   A second child, Timothy is born, and their first child, Abiel, dies.

1768   The Allens move to Bennington, Vermont.

1769   Allen becomes a founding member of the Green Mountain Boys.

1771   Allen and his friend Thomas Ashley build shanties and are the first settlers in Poultney, Vermont.

1775   Allen is one of eighty-five men, including Ethan Allen and Benedict Arnold, to capture a British garrison at Fort Ticonderoga before daybreak and without a shot fired.

1775   Allen moves his family a few miles away to Tinmouth.

1775   Allen enlists eighteen men to join a company of forty-two soldiers to subsequently serve on a five-week scouting mission into Canada.

1776   Allen is chosen as a Tinmouth selectman and delegate, representing Tinmouth at the New Hampshire Convention at Dorset, where Vermont declared freedom from New York and Great Britain.

1776   Allen is chosen as first lieutenant in Warner's (Colonial) regiment.

1776   Allen becomes a captain and a member of Captain Gideon Brownson's detachment for thirty days. The regiment was raised for the immediate defense of the Vermont frontiers.

1777   Allen serves as a delegate to the Windsor, Vermont convention, where the Vermont Constitution was written and signed.

1777   Allen leads a small detachment at the Battle of Bennington to within firing range of an artillery cannon; he kills the gunners and captures the cannon.

1777   Allen is named first captain in Lieutenant Colonel Seth Herrick's Rangers. He is appointed major in Herrick's Rangers by the Vermont Council of Safety.

1777   With forty rangers, Allen scales Mount Defiance, which overlooks Fort Ticonderoga, in the dark; it is defended by two hundred British soldiers and two cannons. The British troops immediately flee and are captured.

1777   Allen blocks British escape during General Burgoyne's surrender at Saratoga, New York, and 5,791 British and German troops are taken as prisoners of war.

Chronology of Ebenezer Allen

1777   While surrounding Fort Ticonderoga with Colonel Brown's Rangers in a stalemate, Allen ties a piece of white cloth to the end of his musket, without a drum or "papers," and approaches the fort to reconnoiter the British garrison.

1777   Allen and his ranger company capture the retreating British rear guard, and he personally emancipates two people who were enslaved by a British officer near Essex, New York.

1777   As a representative at the Vermont Assembly, Allen signs the Vermont Constitution.

1777   Allen introduces an oath of allegiance to the town of Tinmouth to eliminate Tories.

1777–1778   Allen carries out numerous scouting and security missions in Vermont.

1778   Allen raises a force to post at the New Haven (Vergennes) fort.

1778   Allen and Isaac Clark relieve Captain Sawyer in Shelburne at Fort William.

1779   Allen, with Ethan Allen and one hundred men, arrests a number of Loyalists in Cumberland County who refuse to recognize the authority of the Republic of Vermont. Allen receives a grant in Fair Haven and the "Island of Two Heroes." In that year, he builds a log house on the southern tip of South Hero Island.

1779   Allen is chosen as one of the nine members of a Vermont board of war.

1780   At the request of New York governor Clinton, Allen assembles a force of two hundred men at Mount Independence to successfully deter an invading force of "Tories and Indians" led by Sir John Johnson.

1780   Allen variously sites, builds, staffs and commands forts at Pittsford, Castleton and New Haven Vermont.

1780   Allen is awarded the rank of major in Warner's Regiment and colonel in Herrick's Rangers.

1780   Allen's scouting party discovers Major Chris Carleton's fleet and notifies Ethan Allen, who rallies the full Vermont militia to stop Carleton's mission from further Vermont attacks.

1780–1790   Allen provides protective custody for traitor and British secret service agent Justus Sherwood; he facilitates prisoner exchanges.

1781   Allen builds a frame house on his property in what will become South Hero.

1783   Allen opens a public house; he operates a ferry from South Hero to Colchester Point.

1784   Allen is appointed as a proprietor's clerk and justice of the peace in South Hero.

1786–1798   Allen serves as the South Hero town clerk and as a representative in the Vermont Assembly.

1786   Allen is ordered to remove Native American "intruders" who are harassing settlers in the Missisquoi Bay area in Swanton, Vermont.

1791   As a representative of South Hero at the Convention at Bennington, Allen signs an act and resolution to adopt the U.S. Constitution and to admit Vermont to the Union as a state.

1795   Allen spends almost a year in the Midwest and participates in a scheme to buy land on the Michigan Lower Peninsula from Native Americans, which includes some unethical political components and fails.

1800 Allen moves to Burlington, Vermont, where he runs a tavern at the south wharf.

March 26, 1806 Ebenezer Allen dies in Burlington at the age of sixty-three.

FOREWORD

Throughout my long career in state government, I was fortunate to become well acquainted with Vermont's people, places and history. As I suggest in my memoir, *The Vermont Way*, I've learned that we have only begun to scratch the surface of our storied past. In his book, *Vermont's Ebenezer Allen: Patriot, Commando and Emancipator*, Glenn Fay has dug deep into the life of a remarkable character who played a prominent role in forming the state we know today.

Whether you are a general reader or seasoned historian, you will appreciate his work. Fay approaches this insightful biography as the educator he is and carefully unravels the complexities of life in the 1700s. He delves into the personal relationships, events, triumphs and hardships of that early period in our nascent democracy.

Vermont's Ebenezer Allen engages us in the journey of a man best known as the owner of the tavern where General Ethan Allen spent one of the last nights of his life. But Colonel Ebenezer Allen was, in some ways, more intriguing than his cousins Ethan and Ira, who are widely considered the founders of Vermont. From humble beginnings in Northampton and New Marlborough, Massachusetts, Ebenezer was a charter member of the Green Mountain Boys and among the eighty-three men who, with Ethan and Benedict Arnold, captured Fort Ticonderoga. With Seth Warner, Ebenezer helped seize Crown Point. As a captain in Herrick's Rangers, Ebenezer led an audacious capture of Mount Defiance, which was held by two hundred British soldiers with two cannons. Ebenezer's unit later detained the British rearguard on their retreat to Canada, along with boats, horses, oxen and provisions. Colleagues recounted his harrowing, heroic role at the Battle of Bennington. Later, Ebenezer's unit served at Burgoyne's capitulation at Saratoga. Historians note that Ebenezer and Herrick's Rangers were well known and feared throughout the British army; several say that Ebenezer's courage and skill played a role in the victory at Bennington, which fueled momentum for further Patriot success and, ultimately, the British surrender.

But this biography goes beyond war stories. Among the captured in the rearguard were two enslaved people who were owned by a British officer. Ebenezer hand-wrote an emancipation statement, recorded it at the Bennington Town Clerk's Office and set the enslaved people free. Ebenezer spoke several Native American languages fluently. He was among the signers of Vermont's declaration of independence and its first constitution. He founded two Vermont towns and served multiple terms as a justice of the peace, selectman and legislator over a twenty-year span.

After the war, Ebenezer succeeded as a businessman and public servant. Anecdotes suggest that he related to people of different nations and social classes. He entertained King George III's son Prince Edward, his "mistress" and an entourage at his South Hero tavern. Although he was not a prolific self-promoter, as were some of his countrymen, he left a legacy of charismatic and successful service to his state and country.

This book will be of interest to us New Englanders, but it will also draw lovers of history everywhere. It describes an America before laws, order and justice, when Patriots, Tories and Native Americans were living on the edge of the frontier, teetering between life and death. Although the story takes place in the Northeast, it synchronizes with events in Quebec, Boston and New York City. As Fay peels back the layers of Colonel Allen's life journey, he teases us with some mysteries. History is, of course, filtered through the lens of the storyteller; Fay reserves judgment, but he poses some interesting questions for us to consider that challenge us to contemplate our past, present and future.

James H. Douglas
Governor of Vermont, 2003–2011
Middlebury, Vermont

Preface

Once upon a time, there lived a man of uncommon strength, vigor, courage and conviction, who possessed a benevolent heart of gold, worked honest days and nights and served his town and state in building a democracy. He alarmed adversaries and inspired his allies. He charged into the fire and fury of enemy combatants in fierce battles and freed enslaved people. He befriended Native Americans with fluency in their own languages and hosted British royalty at his inn. He left behind a legacy of hard work, courage, conviction and virtue that is hard to fathom—much less imitate—today.

Once the American Revolution was won, this man, Colonel Ebenezer Allen, established a successful village on an island in the sometimes inhospitable political and seasonal climate of northern Vermont. He was the forefather, enforcer and arbiter of good and evil in a savage, unpredictable and difficult world. But this account is not a whitewashed biography of a legend who becomes more heroic with age. As you shall see, the story doesn't hide the darker events of his life.

A few years ago, I had the good fortune to live on Colonel Allen's property in Two Heroes, now called South Hero. I swam on his beach, walked his paths and imagined his tavern next door. That experience planted curiosity to learn more about this mysterious long-gone legend. Once I had the luxury of time to dig deeper into his past, I found myself once again drawn to his mystique. It started with a phone call from a fellow amateur historian John Devino, president of the Ethan Allen Homestead Board of Directors. He asked, "Do you know of anyone who could do a lecture on Ebenezer Allen for the museum's monthly lecture series?"

After coming up empty-handed for an expert on Colonel Allen, I realized it was my turn. My research began, and I quickly realized what every historical researcher must find. That is, when we start digging into the past, we open doors to fascinating people and events. We find things that reinforce human virtue, and we find deeper mysteries. We also find that the past was much more complicated than we thought.

ACKNOWLEDGEMENTS

I t was a welcome surprise to find enthusiastic historians who were open to share their ideas, work, resources and collections with me. Thank you to Dan O'Neil at the Ethan Allen Homestead Museum for his support and know-how. Thank you to local historical society directors Teresa Robinson at South Hero, Lucille Campbell at Grand Isle and Mary Jane Healy at North Hero, who graciously supported this project. Author Bill Powers, the president of the Pittsford Historical Society, shared his unpublished manuscripts and a small library of documents, images, collections, resources and advice. Thank you to Jerry Mullen at Colonel Seth Warner's Extra-Continental Regiment for sharing his own journal articles and enlightening me on numerous occasions. Thank you to the pandemic-era swamped archivists Prudence Doherty at UVM Special Collections, Mariessa Dobrick at the Vermont State Archives and others who unearthed and shared numerous two-hundred-year-old documents. Thank you to Tinmouth town clerk Gail Fallar for graciously sharing *Tinmouth Channel* articles, Bennington town clerk Cassandra Barbeau and Alburgh assistant town clerk Danielle James for going out of her way to help me when I was in a pinch. Thank you, Miranda Peters, the vice-president of collections, and curator Matt Keagle at Fort Ticonderoga and the friendly folks at the Burlington City Clerk's Office. Thank you to Governor James Douglas, Paul Gillies, Kevin Graffagnino, Michael Bellesiles, Grant Reynolds, Paul Carnahan and Alan Berolzheimer at the Vermont Historical Society, Professor Harvey Amani Whitfield, Ed Steele, John Buttolph, Herman "Charlie" Brown, Dawn

ACKNOWLEDGEMENTS

Hance, Bob Underhill, David Cawley, Robert Blanchard, Joseph Perron, David Blow, Sheriff Roger Langevin, Jay Barney and Joe Citro. Thank you to my copyeditor, Ashley Hill, and Mike Kinsella at Arcadia Publishing and The History Press for their generous time, conversations and coaching from ideas to fruition. Finally, thank you to my wife, Donna, who has been my reality checker and guide throughout my research and writing.

INTRODUCTION

Two young men pulled their heavy dugout canoe onto the rugged rocky shoreline in the protection of a point of land during the storm, shielding them from the crashing waves. It was a cold, gray, blustery day in September 1783. They had paddled along six miles of shoreline from Jed's cabin, looking for meat. Dr. Davis had said that he had some pork, but he was out, too. And before that, they had previously paddled ten miles from the island farther north. Despite it being the harvest season, meat was scarce. The new settlers had recently arrived, and many had not found sufficient time to establish gardens and orchards—not to mention herds of livestock and chickens. They were also behind on storing meat and fish. Many of the residents would be eating only bread and milk during the coming winter.

Living on an island meant that livestock had to be brought to a new home over the ice during the area's brutal winters; a few animals could also be brought over on a small wooden ferry. Breeding a herd could take years. Ferry trips were dependent on warmer weather, and they were often adventure-filled excursions to say the least. The settlers were living in a frontier of thick, dense wilderness. Moving anywhere on land meant walking or riding on horseback over sometimes dense, rocky or swampy terrain. Without roads, the main transportation and communication source was dugout canoes.

In 1783, a dozen log homes and barns and a couple of wood-frame houses dotted the fourteen-mile long island. The earliest White settlers, Colonel Ebenezer Allen, Alexander Gordon and Jed's father, Captain Jedediah Hyde, had only built homes a couple of years earlier. Allen had cleared a few acres of the dense forest and planted wheat, vegetables and a few apple trees. He was one of the go-to guys for provisions and survival know-how.

As the founding father of the island, forty-year-old Colonel Allen was their last hope for finding meat that day. As Jed and his friend arrived at Allen's place, just up on a short bluff from the shoreline, they saw several other men outside in the field. Apparently, Allen had gone to get provisions and had not yet returned. Allen's wife had only one salmon to offer the hungry neighbors. Jed and David decided to fend for themselves; they sharpened their axes and pushed the canoe out into the waves with the hope of catching more fish.

A few yards from the shoreline, the canoe swamped in the big rolling waves of the broad lake, and both men were drenched. Fishing would have to wait another day. They rescued their gear, bailed out the water and pulled the canoe up on the beach again. They knew they would need to dry their clothes inside or risk getting sick. Once they were in the Allens' house, they dried off by the fire, and Mrs. Allen cooked half of the salmon for the visitors. They had tea, then some punch and then they went to bed. In the morning, the two men cut firewood to repay the Allens for their hospitality. They often saw deer, which were usually very timid and elusive.

It was Jed who spotted the hulking black shape in the woods, moving away from them—a black bear. They didn't have their guns, and the animal disappeared quickly, padding into a thicket of evergreens. They often saw deer, and they were usually very fast and elusive. Only a seasoned woodsman could get close enough to get a shot off to hit one. Squirrels were plentiful, as were geese, ducks and other shorebirds, especially in the spring and fall. But animal meat didn't keep for long unless it was smoked or salted.

Food wasn't the only commodity that was scarce on the island. Many had very little clothing, and some had worn out their shoes. They didn't have the raw materials to make their own clothes, and the closest store was in Bennington, which was several days away on horseback. The closest mills for grinding flour and sawing logs were days away by boat in New York State. Some of the larger towns, such as Bennington, had provisions that were available to buy, but one needed currency or products to trade or barter. American dollars were few and far between, and they were often of questionable value. It would take years of new settlers bringing their resources, know-how and resilience to build a stronger and healthier local community.

1

HARD LIVING AND FAITH

Ebenezer Allen was a major-league celebrity during his lifetime; he was widely known in the Northeast and was feared by the northern British army. Allen accomplished more militarily and personally in a span of eight years, from 1775 to 1783, than most high achievers do in a lifetime. During those years, he pulled off some astonishing accomplishments. Even if we ignore his military achievements, we find that Allen also lived a robust and adventurous life before and after the American Revolution.

Most Vermonters know that brothers Ethan and Ira Allen are the traditional Vermont heroes, but most don't know about their cousin Ebenezer, even though he arguably recorded more military and public service accomplishments than Ethan, and he managed to make an honest living and leave life with a full piggy bank. Unlike Ethan and Ira, Ebenezer never wrote an autobiography or sought the limelight. Colonel Ebenezer Allen seemed to possess the same gumption genes as the rest of the notable Allens, and when it came to action, he walked the walk. He was not only a dauntless Patriot with courage and conviction, but also an elite combat commando, a pioneer emancipator and a respected public servant, who shaped the values of the republic and the state of Vermont, both at the grass-roots level and in the big picture.

If you are not a Revolutionary War scholar, keep in mind that in Allen's birth year, 1743, there was no "United States" yet, and it would be almost fifty years before there was a state of Vermont. In general terms, the colonies were largely unceded Native lands, possessed by the British and won from the French and Native people over 150 bloody years. New England was increasingly polarized between the American Patriots and British Loyalists, who were living side by side in the new towns. The Vermont we know today was part of the New Hampshire land grants. In fact, the word *Vermont* had not even been invented yet.

Independent and evolved thinking in Vermont has roots in the American Revolution. And as tempting as it may be, we should not be too quick to judge others from another time by using our own seemingly impeccable hindsight and present-day ethics, since colonials lived in a completely different world from the one we live in today.

Ebenezer's story begins in 1743, when he was born to farmers Samuel and Hanna Miller (Jones) Allen in Northampton, Massachusetts. By the time he was eleven, the family had moved to New Marlboro, Massachusetts. Ebenezer was the fourth child of the family. Three of Ebenezer Allen's siblings were living in southern Vermont when they eventually passed away. It is not known when two of his siblings, Jemima and Rachel, passed. Sometimes, this indicates that they died while they were still young children. See chart 1 for more information on Allen's family. Some of the dates from different genealogical sources are in conflict, but for the most part, they are minor discrepancies. But the genealogical information, as it is, offers a picture of the Allens' own robust family from the 1760s through the end of the century.

We know very little about Allen's formative years, but we do know he was raised in a religious family and lived in the religious town of Northampton; he was baptized by the eminent Calvinist Jonathan Edwards.[1] Edwards was a brilliant prodigy and Puritan theologian, scientist and minister who helped spark the Great Awakening, which was a religious revival of the 1740s that was said to have been a reaction to the Age of Enlightenment of the eighteenth century. The Age of Enlightenment was a movement in politics, philosophy, science and communication that had radically reoriented life in Europe and in the colonies. The Great Awakening followed in several waves and boosted the number of Christians in New England. Reverend Edwards attracted throngs of converts to Northampton for a time. But in the prime of his career, Edwards also attracted intense controversy.

For one thing, Edwards's monotone but descriptive sermons were so convincing with their imagery that some of his parishioners began having visions and speaking in tongues during services, which disrupted others. This alarmed parishioners to the point that they began to question and suspect his practices. In addition, it so happened that Reverend Edwards enslaved three

Reverend Jonathan Edwards baptized Ebenezer Allen in Northampton, Massachusetts. *Public domain.*

African Americans, which was antithetical to the beliefs of many colonists in New England. Not only did Edwards own enslaved people, he also boldly defended human bondage and wrote a paper that steadfastly defended owning people, especially those who were debtors. This is interesting, since Ebenezer Allen would become a believer who did not believe in slavery. In fact, Allen would become the first White man known to publicly emancipate enslaved people in the American colonies.[2]

Edwards had one other distinction. At the time, smallpox was rampant, and the disease was decimating people in the colonies. Most churches had taken a stand against the then-innovative practice of variolation. Variolation was the procedure of removing some discharge from a smallpox sore and inserting it into a cut on another person's skin. Variolation was an early form of vaccination that had success in reducing smallpox infections. But strict fatalist beliefs in some churches held that only God had sovereignty over one's fate. Therefore, interfering with nature should be forbidden. Edwards eventually died as a result of a smallpox inoculation at the age of fifty-five.

Ebenezer's father passed away when he was twelve, in 1755, after recently moving the family. This left Ebenezer, his mother and two older siblings with an arduous farm life in New Marlboro, Massachusetts. New Marlboro's land had been purchased from Mohican (Eastern Algonquin) Natives and was thriving, and the community was growing quickly during the 1740s and 1750s. Allen received little formal education, and although he did learn to read and write, that education probably came from his mother and apprenticeships. We have a slim record of his own writings, but there are some invoices and correspondences with his cousins Levi and Ira Allen that will be revealed in later chapters.

Most estimates of literacy in the eighteenth century depend on the definition of literacy. Some estimates put male literacy as high as 80 percent and female literacy at 50 percent by 1776, which may be higher than it is in the United States today. But Allen did not take any college courses or enjoy any private tutoring as some of his cousins did. Regardless of his lack of formal schooling, he became very skilled in life.

Allen apprenticed briefly with a blacksmith at a young age. In working with a blacksmith, it's possible that he not only learned how to design and make things, but he also may have become acquainted with the way things worked and some of the advanced technology of the day. At that time, blacksmithing was a prestigious profession, and the kings of the trade were often members of the higher class social and political hierarchy. Blacksmithing was in high demand, as blacksmiths made tools and could repair almost everything. The profession relied on engineering and problem-solving skills. Most of the cutting-edge technologies of the 1700s relied on designing, fabricating and repairing metal tools, weapons and home goods. Blacksmithing included the fabrication and repair of much of the essential technology of the day. In addition, blacksmithing necessitated education and required reading, writing and arithmetic.[3]

Allen also became acquainted with the Natives' ways at a young age and spoke three Native American dialects fluently. This helps explain how Allen became a man who felt at home among Native people and found alliances with them. His early life also gives clues about his work ethic, discipline, know-how, brawn, self-reliance and healthy self-esteem.[4]

As a point of reference to some other better-known Patriots, according to Allen's descendant Orrin Peer Allen, Allen and Vermont founder Ethan Allen's great-grandfathers were brothers, meaning Ebenezer and Ethan were cousins. It is unknown if the two men were aware of their relatively close lineage. (See chart 2.)[5] As we shall see, Ethan and Ebenezer frequented many of the same towns and territories, along with several other members of the Allen clan and many others from the Connecticut and Massachusetts colonies.

Ethan was born in 1738 in Connecticut, making him five years older than Ebenezer. The other well-known Vermont founder, Ira Allen, wouldn't be born until 1751, making Ebenezer eight years older than him, although the paper trail of military service and letters shows they were close acquaintances and crossed paths frequently. We also know that Ebenezer lived by some religious convictions and that Ethan did not. Although we have not found a record of Ebenezer's frequent church attendance, his actions and verbal attributions allude to his adherence to Protestant principles.

The Allen clan was prominent in colonial America, and in general, families at this time tended to have eight or more children. Some of the Allens in Vermont were known to have been related to one another and some were not. The characters in this biography include Ebenezer's cousins, children and unrelated colleagues. They all serve as a context for our main character, and the author refers to Ebenezer as "Allen" throughout the story.

As Allen matured, he became an alert and physically powerful young man who was full of strong convictions and intensely pursued a better life. For Allen and others in Connecticut, New York and the Massachusetts Bay Colony, the land of opportunity appeared to be waiting in the great wilderness to the north of Massachusetts.

2

BARE-KNUCKLE PATRIOTISM

In 1762, at the age of nineteen, Allen married the sixteen-year-old Lydia Richards, a New Marlboro native. Although not much is recorded of Richards's family history or her early matrimony with Ebenezer, we know that her parents were Zebulon Richards and Lydia (Brown) Richards, and they were also from New Marlboro. By 1768, the Allens had produced four children, but two may have died by then. Some accounts say they moved to Bennington for a couple of years. By then, Bennington had a sawmill and a gristmill and was a booming village with plenty of opportunities for work and farming. Ethan Allen lived in Old Bennington between 1769 until 1775, and it is possible that Ethan helped Ebenezer become established. At that time, Ebenezer's vociferous cousin Ethan Allen had just been banished from Salisbury, Connecticut, and Northampton for getting variolated without town permission and antagonizing church beliefs.[6]

As we shall see, although taking the lord's name in vain and using vernacular language was common parlance with many men of the time, that wasn't Allen's style. His surviving handwritten letters often show poor grammar, usage and mechanics, but he kept his lingo clean. Even though his writing was rudimentary, some of his documents, such as his Tinmouth loyalty pledge and his emancipation statement, show a fair amount of sophistication that would have resulted from revisions. Like other writers, he apparently revised and rewrote some of his correspondences.

We also know that Allen served as a tithing man in Tinmouth and on a committee to find and hire a (Congregational) minister in South Hero, the community where he and his family lived the longest (twenty years). But the communities Allen founded did not have organized churches—at least early on. Many of the founders were trying to escape rigid Puritanical churches, and they weren't eager to reestablish formal churches. It appears that Allen was one of those men who espoused Christian virtues even though he was not a formal Sunday worshipper. According to firsthand accounts, he was an honest and kind-hearted man, which, at the time, were considered to be Christian virtues, and after his death, he was given a Masonic, instead of a Christian, funeral.

Life in the New Hampshire land grants during the later 1700s was difficult, at best, for a lot of reasons. First, survival in colonial America before germ theory became common knowledge was risky. Most people lived in close quarters with poor nutrition, lack of personal hygiene and what we might consider counterproductive medical practices and medications. Allen and his wife lost at least one of their ten children at a young age. Their firstborn, Abiel, only lived to be two years old and died in 1765. Why were mortality rates so high in the eighteenth century?

For one thing, few people gave a second thought to the disease-creating capacity of rotting food, human waste from chamber pots dumped in streets, common sewers, stagnant ponds, privies and other places. In cities, sewage was commonly dumped near the streets, where it eventually mixed with effluent from slaughterhouses and storm runoff, which eventually drained into rivers, ponds and lakes. Since any body of water could be a source of drinking water, pathogens were pervasive. It wasn't until the mid- to late 1800s that municipal sewage systems were built. But other febrile (fever-producing) diseases decimated populations around the time that Ebenezer Allen was born. Scarlet fever was one of them.

New England, along with the rest of the colonies, was full of diseases in the 1700s. Abiel Allen might have succumbed to any number of diseases, including smallpox, influenza, pneumonia, throat distemper (later sorted and identified as either scarlet fever or diphtheria) and measles.[7] The last three were common childhood epidemics in the New England colonies and frequently led to complications and death. But during the 1700s, physicians believed that all febrile illnesses resulted from an excess of stimulation and excitement of the blood. Therefore, they believed purging would divert the force of the fever to the bowels and save the liver and brain from fatal congestion. Some febrile diseases, such as malaria and yellow fever, turned out to be caused by mosquitoes in the warmer colonies, while other diseases turned out to be caused by microbes in raw sewage or other putrid substances. But the causes would not be sorted out until the 1800s, and at that time, the treatments for febrile diseases were largely the same.

Scarlet fever symptoms include sore throat, high fever, enlarged tonsils, headache and a body rash. Victims sometimes died within forty-eight hours. The symptoms overlap a variety of other diseases, and the fever sometimes leads to pneumonia, kidney disease, rheumatic heart disease, arthritis and rheumatic fever. Scarlet fever is caused by streptococcus bacteria and spreads through coughs, sneezes and contact with others. It begins with "strep throat," and the bacteria produce toxins that damage plasma membranes of blood capillaries under the skin. This produces the characteristic red rash on the body and tongue known as strawberry tongue, which distinguishes scarlet fever from other diseases.

Fevers in the 1700s were commonly treated by bloodletting from a vein under the tongue or in the arm, a borax and honey throat wash, a "plaster" to burn the throat or create skin blisters on the body, physicks (purging the bowels) and various other remedies. The purpose of these treatments was to redirect the fever away from the brain, throat and larynx and promote healing.[8] Doctors used stomach plasters, saline purgatives, cordials and wine with antiemetics (nausea suppressants) to control gastrointestinal symptoms of these diseases. Eventually, some of the doctors noticed that some of the treatments were more dangerous than the diseases themselves.

The good news for the Allens was that most of their children survived into adulthood and had successful lives. Allen's daughter Charlotte married a man named Melvin Barnes. Their son Dr. Melvin Barnes Jr. grew up in Grand Isle, near Ebenezer, and later lived in the neighboring town of Alburgh. Melvin Barnes Jr. is noteworthy, as he published a brief biography of Allen in 1852. Barnes was born in 1794, so he would have known his grandfather quite well before the elder died in 1806. Allen's son Timothy served as a colonel in the Revolutionary War, became active in South Hero, Vermont town affairs and served several terms as a representative to the Vermont Assembly.[9] In his later years, Timothy moved to Constable, New York, where he died. Another Allen son, Ebenezer Walbridge Allen, lived in Indiana, where he later passed away.

THE POLARIZED POLITICAL CLIMATE IN EARLY NEW HAMPSHIRE

In 1741, Benning Wentworth, who was a shipping merchant in Portsmouth, New Hampshire, had recently become the governor of that colony. By 1749, Wentworth would take the audacious step of selling a six-mile parcel of land, with twenty-four thousand acres, west of the Connecticut River and presumably in the New York Colony, to Colonel William Williams and fifty-nine other grantees. In fact, Wentworth decided to name the town after himself (Bennington), and he granted five hundred acres in that town to himself. During the next decade, Wentworth repeated this, and granted scores of six-square-mile towns in what would eventually become Vermont. The shrewd and cheeky Wentworth would often name the towns after historic English royalty despite the vehement protests of then–New York governor George Clinton. In a matter of years, Allen moved to the thriving town of Bennington with his young family and got his start with the Green Mountain Boys.

A 1764 order from King George III of England stated that the province of New York extended to the Connecticut River. As a result, in the 1770s, New York's governors had good reason to believe that property between Lake Champlain and the Connecticut River was legally within their domain. Therefore, British army general and governor William Tryon, from 1771 to 1777, made a concerted effort to control the settlements in that territory, although New Hampshire governor Wentworth was actively granting property to himself and other settlers. The New York titles led to most of the towns in the region of southern Vermont becoming inhabited by Loyalists, many of whom came from New York, and American Patriots, who migrated from Connecticut and Massachusetts and counted on the New Hampshire land grants being valid.

Although the British believed New York had legal authority over the New Hampshire Grants, the majority of

Benning Wentworth was the governor of New Hampshire. *Public domain.*

Right: George Clinton was the governor of New York. *Public domain.*

Opposite: King George III was the king of Great Britain. *Public domain.*

White settlers were taking advantage of the New Hampshire land deeds to buy affordable land. New Yorkers tended to be Loyalists who supported the king, and as such, property was distributed to wealthy manor lords and then rented out to settlers without amenities, such as churches and schools. This model was contrary to the philosophy of many new Vermonters. New York leaders persisted in surveying New Hampshire (later to become Vermont) territory and sending settlers to populate the towns, despite the fact that New Hampshire grant holders had, in many cases, already bought land and built homesteads.

Although the terms *Loyalist*—those colonists who felt loyalty to the British Crown—and *Tory* may have slightly different connotations for some, the author of this book will use the terms interchangeably.

A BENNINGTON MILITIA HOLDS OFF YORKERS

A Bennington militia had been formed as far back as 1764, after New York authorities issued arrest warrants for some "rioters" in the New Hampshire territory. According to Duffy, Muller and Shattuck, in their book *The Rebel and the Tory*, the New York government sought to extend its control over the region by insisting the New Hampshire grantees pay them fees to secure

legal land titles from New York. Many New Hampshire grantees objected to paying a second fee for their land titles, and they resisted New York control.

In 1769, an Albany (New York) sheriff arrived in Bennington to subdivide the land of James Breakenridge, who possessed a New Hampshire grant. A large group of Bennington militiamen arrived to take over and fortify Breakenridge's house. This forced the sheriff to reevaluate his priorities and return to New York State. Shortly thereafter, in 1769, the New Hampshire Green Mountain Boys militia group was officially established by Ethan Allen. Ebenezer Allen was a charter and active member in that rowdy roughhousing group. New York's persistent efforts to exert control culminated in the 1770–71 ejectment trials in New York to enforce their legal rights and land titles on those grantees.[10]

Scholars point out that some of the common beliefs about the Green Mountain Boys, sometimes called the Mob or the Boys, may not be very accurate. Historian Donald Smith showed that the Green Mountain Boys were "highly motivated social activists of significant political experience and vision" before they even came to Vermont.[11] He says they were not youthful, profane, hard-drinking, irreligious adventurers like Ethan Allen, but rather, they were highly motivated and experienced economic, political and religious activists. Smith notes that many of the 436 Green Mountain Boys had experience as New York rioters with social activism experience.

According to Smith, hundreds of western Vermont migrants had previously moved to New York to escape religious persecution in Massachusetts during the Great Awakening. As the New Yorkers adhered to a conservative social organization, the Boys adopted a more progressive mentality. Although New York may have been free from religious persecution, the migrants had soon become disenfranchised with the socioeconomic institutions of the "manor lords" and created a land war. They hated the New Yorkers, also known as "Yorkers," for their social institutions, not for any cultural differences.

Smith contends that Ethan Allen capitalized on the Boys' beliefs and experiences instead of motivating them to action, as has been portrayed. Ethan also followed his younger brother Ira's path toward land speculation, which was entirely founded on the authenticity of New Hampshire land grants. Ethan had a personal financial stake in keeping New York out of New Hampshire's (Vermont) real estate.[12] Although we don't know if Allen yearned to escape the Great Awakening, as some of his brethren in the Boys did, he certainly fits the profile of an activist with spiritual convictions who was ready to fight for freedom.

Patriot, Commando and Emancipator

General Ira Allen was a founder of Vermont and UVM. *Public domain.*

As a result of the conflicting land deeds, buying or trading land parcels using New York patents or New Hampshire deeds from either colony was risky. Most of the territory was still wilderness that was occupied and used by Natives, and plenty of British Loyalists lived among others who had strong American revolutionary sentiments. But by the early 1770s, the so-called British colonies were undergoing a radical and unstoppable change.

The 1770 Boston Massacre, in which several American protesters and bystanders were killed by British soldiers in reaction to a protest, had galvanized American opposition in Boston to British rule. Several other skirmishes in the Boston area, such as the bloodshed at Lexington and Concord, tax revolts and the occupation by British troops would accelerate conflicts between the British and the "rebels," who increasingly wanted freedom from the king's rule. The wave of anti-British sentiment intensified and spread northward into the New Hampshire colony.

Although the Boys were not aiming to be a mainstream military combat company, their unorthodox fortitude left no doubt in the minds of their opponents that they were ready to do anything necessary to protect their land. They were successful at intimidating and roughing up New York Loyalists on what would become Vermont soil. They were, in fact, a Vermont minuteman militia; they were true Patriots, unlike those who often co-opt the use of the term today. The Green Mountain Boys embodied patriotism, and devoted Patriots, at the time, were defined by their fervent desire and willingness to fight for independence from Britain and, especially, the Loyalist-leaning Yorkers.

Several towns in southern Vermont, especially Bennington, served as the headquarters for the Green Mountain Boys. In fact, the Green Mountain Tavern was later called the Catamount Tavern in Old Bennington, which had been built in the mid-1760s by Stephen Fay. The tavern, like other taverns of the time, was the site of many meetings, and plans were made there to resist what the Green Mountain Boys saw as the tyranny of New York and King George III of Great Britain.

The Green Mountain Boys had a reputation of drinking and scheming long into the night, but this portrayal may not be entirely accurate. Granted, the meeting places of the day were often taverns, and although Ethan Allen had a well-documented love of alcohol, according to historian Smith, ideology fueled the rebellion more than alcohol. Alcohol was commonplace in the colonies, as it was part of the average diet—not to mention its social and medicinal use. Over a few years, the Boys organized a tight network of minutemen who stood ready to respond to all kinds of security issues.

Today, the site of the tavern in Old Town Bennington is surrounded by Revolutionary War–period architecture. The tavern is within eye shot of the former town center and the present location of the towering Bennington Monument, which commemorates the Battle of Bennington that occurred a few miles away.

Most of the Boys lived in Bennington or neighboring towns, such as Arlington, Manchester and Windsor, and eventually, they settled even farther north in Tinmouth and Poultney. They typically had families, farms and businesses and left their wives and kids at home to survive while they were away. In some cases, small detachments of Boys would go on missions that could take them anywhere in the southern Vermont–New Hampshire area or across the border into New York State. These operations included "scouting" missions, and more often they responded to Yorker sheriffs, surveyors or Tories who were, as far as they were concerned, stepping on their turf. Many of these missions included violent overtones, especially with Ethan Allen's well-documented boisterous rhetoric and threats.

Throughout his life, Ebenezer Allen was involved in a lot of scouting missions, both with the Green Mountain Boys and the military. Scouting was a term used for missions of intelligence-gathering, in which they would determine enemy positions or plans, conduct light or sporadic combat to delay enemy movement, disrupt enemy attacks or otherwise make their opponent's lives miserable. Allen knew his way around the different types of muskets, rifles and other weaponry—he also knew his way around the woodlands. As we shall see, he stood out and was charismatic enough to quickly be drafted as an officer in the militias when the time came.

The populations of the southern towns enjoyed a steady influx of new settlers, some of whom staked a claim, built a shanty and left and others who intended to stay and settle down. In general, colonial Americans moved around the new frontier for all kinds of reasons. Historians often claim that a chief reason was to settle near family members and friends. Finding success on the northern frontier meant farming the land, building, logging and setting up businesses, trade and land speculation opportunities. Properties near bodies of water offered the fastest transportation and, sometimes, the energy to drive sawmills for wood or gristmills for grain. And during that time, the best opportunities to find cheap acreage lay northward, in the New Hampshire land grants.

ALLEN STAKES CLAIMS

In 1771, Allen, along with his friend and fellow Green Mountain Boy Thomas Ashley, who had married Lydia Richards Allen's sister Zeruiah Richards, struck out northward, bought pitches of New Hampshire land and built shanties in Poultney. They are credited with being the first settlers who established that town. Allen and Ashley were bold and fearless spirits, ready to conquer their world. The two started a settlement by building shanties near the turnpike bridge in what is now West Poultney. The shanties consisted of four crotched posts set in the ground, more poles placed on the top and a roof and sides covered with bark. Setting up homes near the river seemed like a good idea at the time. During their first night, April 15, 1771, on the south bank of the Poultney River, a heavy deluge ensued. The river slowly but surely rose during the night and flooded them out. They had to retreat in the darkness to a nearby hill, where they started over.[13]

A majority of the Poultney grantees were former residents of Litchfield County, Connecticut, and Berkshire County, Massachusetts, where Allen was born. As in other New Hampshire towns, the grantees were required to pay "the rent of one ear of Indian corn only, on the 25th day of December, annually," for ten years and one shilling per one hundred acres held thereafter. The proprietors were also required to cultivate five acres for every fifty acres they owned and reserve large white and other pines for masts for the Royal Navy.[14]

Allen worked as a surveyor, and in June 1773, he was surveying in nearby Tinmouth. He apparently fell in love with a very nice pitch near the mouth of the Poultney River, in an area known as the Gulf. By September 1774, he had moved his family there. He had an interest and experience in farming and in the seemingly endless supply of forests for timber trade and land investments. He also wanted to explore the vast far-northern wilderness. His daughter Vashti Allen was born in Ontario, Canada, in 1774, possibly while

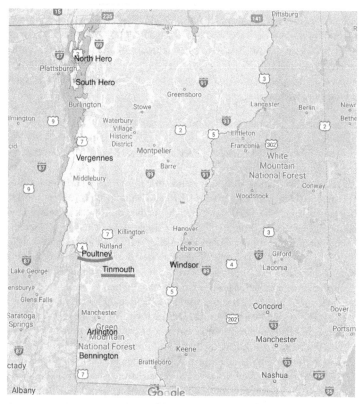

Bennington, Poultney, Tinmouth, South Hero and Burlington were all towns where Ebenezer and Lydia Allen lived. *Courtesy of Google Maps.*

Allen was traveling on an expedition. Unlike his cousin Ethan, Allen appears to have consistently stayed in Vermont year-round instead of retreating to Connecticut during the colder months. His family lived in Tinmouth until at least 1780.

According to Tinmouth historian Grant Reynolds, Allen's farm sat on today's Vermont 140, about three miles west of Tinmouth Village. His brothers also bought land and settled nearby, and Ethan Allen owned three hundred acres next to Allen, which he eventually sold in Litchfield, Connecticut, two weeks after he was released from British captivity in 1778.[15]

Those of us who are fortunate enough to live in rural Vermont today are acquainted with the aesthetic splendor of the state's hills and valleys, the wildlife and, perhaps, the regenerative effects of forest bathing. But during the eighteenth century, the Vermont woods still had a healthy population of large predators, such as mountain lions, bears and wolves. As settlers invaded their territory, it was only natural that confrontations occurred. For the first time in North America, native animals were being forced to adapt to humans, who were clearing their old-growth forest habitat and hunting them on a larger scale.

Allen quickly became active in Tinmouth, where he was chosen as the town highway surveyor, fence viewer and tithingman. A tithingman was a common position in the Congregational Church in the New Hampshire colony, and as such, Allen was an official who was responsible for patrolling road traffic on the Sabbath. Tithingmen were selected to detain and arrest people and ensure that people were either traveling to church, attending to the sick or doing charitable work on the Sabbath. Tithingmen could also quiet loud people or wake sleepers during a church service. In some towns, tithingmen arrested people and unruly kids and placed them in stocks as punishment. This offers another clue of Allen's beliefs and temperament. Of course, while fulfilling his duties as a tithingman, it would be difficult for him to fully enjoy the sermons and all that the church services had to offer.[16]

Allen's family had grown, and his oldest children would have been older than ten at the time and able to help with household chores and farming. Even though Tinmouth was the Allen family's residence and civic base for three years, the Revolution was heating up, and the record shows, as we shall see, that Allen was not much of a homebody.

Although the mountainous town of Tinmouth was settled in 1761, it was only four square miles in area, with five hundred acres set aside for His Excellency, Benning Wentworth, the governor of New Hampshire. Ten-acre shares were also set aside for the Church of England, a parsonage and a school. Two rivers, the Tinmouth and Poultney Rivers, both flowed through the town and provided waterpower. The town established that it would organize and have its first town meeting the following year, 1772. However, there was much work to be done, and this meeting didn't actually happen until 1774.

In 1776, the inhabitants voted to build a log house for religious services on the Sabbath. Reverend Obadiah Noble was the first preacher, and the inhabitants voted to build a meetinghouse in 1779. Noble, who had graduated from New Jersey College, had also been a Congregational minister before moving to Tinmouth. He served for many years as clerk of the court in Rutland County and as justice of the peace in Tinmouth.

Tinmouth was selected as a shire town, or government seat, and courts were conducted at the inn of Solomon Bingham (who was also a blacksmith) from 1781 to 1784. The court and tavern business was held in one room, and the family's living room was in the other. When the jury was to deliberate, they moved to a log barn about fifty paces away. A mile down the path from the courtroom was the county jail, which had a blanket hung up to serve as a door.[17]

Life was good in the growing community of Tinmouth, but there were alarms and raids happening all around them in Vermont, and the battles a couple of hundred miles south, in Boston, were gaining more attention with every passing month. The cries for independence became louder. But there were plenty of Loyalists who seemed content with British rule, and some of them were living among Allen and other Patriots who were rebelling against King George III. And that became increasingly dangerous for the Patriot settlers.

SURPRISE MILITARY STRIKES

The Green Mountain Boys carried out a lot of well-documented interventions in the early 1770s as they quickly reacted to the New York governor's strong-arm enforcement activities. The Boys prevented surveyors and sheriffs from carrying out their orders and duties, took cattle, burned down the buildings of "unauthorized" settlers who didn't have New Hampshire deeds and administered floggings and other punishments—they even hanged a traitor after their own trial, with Ethan Allen acting as the judge.

Meanwhile, a major sea change was underway in the colonies. The accounts of the Battles of Lexington and Concord on April 18 and 19, 1775, were heard loud and clear in places like Tinmouth, and settlers were outraged. On June 17, one hundred Americans were killed and three hundred were wounded at Bunker Hill. Allen joined a town militia that was formed later that month and Warner's (Continental) regiment at the same time. He helped the town procure a store of gunpowder and was well-connected and experienced from his work with the Green Mountain Boys. Allen was commissioned with an officer's rank of lieutenant in Warner's Rangers.

In early May, Allen's cousin Ethan was looking for a group of men for a secret mission, and this stoked anti-British sentiment further. Allen and a bunch of others from Tinmouth signed up. The mission was so secret that no one—not even the soldiers' wives—knew where they were headed. John Spafford's wife, Mary Baldwin Spafford, later recalled how she was very

Left: Benedict Arnold co-commanded the capture of Fort Ticonderoga with Ethan Allen but later became a traitor. *Courtesy of the National Archives.*

Right: Ethan Allen Hitchcock, Ethan Allen's grandson by his daughter Lucy, was said to be a dead ringer look-alike of Ethan Allen. *Public domain.*

concerned that her husband had left with his gun and a few provisions in his backpack during the first week of May. At the time, he couldn't give her a time frame for the mission, but he didn't return for three weeks.[18]

On May 10, 1775, Allen was one of eighty-three men on that mission, led by Ethan Allen and Benedict Arnold, who captured Fort Ticonderoga before daybreak. Most accounts of this Green Mountain Boys mission agree that it was risky, and Allen's forces were not well prepared. The attack was also complicated by the fact that the Massachusetts Council of Safety had ordered Colonel Benedict Arnold to capture the fort a couple of days before.

Arnold recruited some troops, then raced ahead to catch Allen and his Green Mountain Boys at Castleton, which was their staging area for the attack. This was a world-class clash of egos, and it lived up to its potential. Allen had his mind made up that it was his intel, his plan, his men and his opportunity. Arnold was equally hungry for success and advancement, and he had orders, the credentials, dress uniforms and a bull-headed drive that were only matched by Allen's own ego. Colonel Ethan Allen and Colonel Benedict Arnold both made their own personal cases to lead the group, and in the end, many of the Green Mountain Boys said they would go home

An aerial view of present-day Fort Ticonderoga. *Courtesy of Fort Ticonderoga.*

rather than be commanded by anyone other than Ethan Allen. After an emotional confrontation, the two worked out some measure of compromise to jointly command the attack.

Although Ethan had sent two soldiers disguised as fur trappers ahead to reconnoiter the situation inside the fort and others to procure boats to cross the lake, only one boat had arrived on the Vermont shore by 1:30 a.m. Arnold and Allen were only able to move eighty-three men across the lake in the darkness. And as it was, they were running out of darkness and were fearful of losing the element of surprise. They also feared that British reinforcements were on the way. Only a portion of the several hundred Patriots were on hand to attack, and these men had marched, prepped and stayed up all night, waiting for the transportation to arrive. But the eighty-three Patriots on the New York shoreline were hungry for victory, and they had the element of surprise.

On storming into the old stone fort, one account says the men enjoyed good fortune when a sentry's rifle misfired—it had been aimed at Ethan. Ethan's account claims his men shouted three cheers and he whacked a second sentry with the side of his sword to avoid decapitating him.[19] With

Arnold and Allen in the forefront, the 83 jacked-up Green Mountain Boys disarmed the 140 sleepy British soldiers. Ethan Allen met Captain Delaplace face to face at his doorway and demanded a surrender. The British didn't have a chance.

Ebenezer Allen was right behind Ethan, one of the eighty-three men leading the attack. The rest of the group included Seth Warner; Thomas Ashley; Matthew Lyon; John Spafford; Benjamin Wait and his brothers; Samuel Herrick (who also captured Skenesborough); Remember Baker (who simultaneously intercepted spies on Otter Creek that were attempting to pass on the information that Fort Ticonderoga had fallen); John Kennedy Sr.; and John Kennedy Jr. Both Kennedys claimed to have been by Ethan Allen's side at the top of the stairs when the British commander, Delaplace, surrendered. The younger Kennedy said Delaplace had come to his door with his breeches in hand, and he said that he "would never forget the look on his pale face or his naked legs."[20] Eventually, over four hundred American Patriots arrived at the fort and ransacked and pillaged its large quantities of food, rum and supplies, much to the chagrin of Colonel Arnold, who was extremely concerned about the lack of discipline and decorum among the Green Mountain Boys.

Fort Ticonderoga's barracks. *Courtesy of Fort Ticonderoga.*

As soon as Fort Ticonderoga was under control, Ebenezer Allen was one of a small detachment, led by Captain Seth Warner, that sailed northward, into strong headwinds, twelve miles up the lake to the fort at Crown Point, where they easily overpowered a small unit and captured their weapons.

The Crown Point haul included:

	Weight (pounds)
One hundred cannons, including:	
Two brass Cohorns (small Howitzers)	300
Four brass Cohorns	400
Two brass mortars	600
One iron mortar	600
Two iron mortars	3,600
Three iron mortars	6,900
Eight brass three-pounder cannons	28,000
Three brass six-pounder cannons	1,800
One brass eighteen-pounder cannon	1,200
One brass twenty-four-pounder cannon	1,800
Six iron six-pounder cannons	15,000
Four iron nine-pounder cannons	10,000
Ten iron twelve-pounder cannons	28,000
Three other cannons	15,000
Two Iron Howitzers	2,000

The haul also included a sergeant and twelve men.

The spoils from the capture of Fort Ticonderoga were even more impressive. A partial list includes eighteen barrels of pork with peas, beans and other provisions. Ninety gallons of rum were not listed in the official record, but it is assumed that all of the rum was drunk posthaste.

The prisoners included Captain Delaplace, Lieutenant Feltham, a conductor of artillery, a gunner, two sergeants and forty-four privates—sixty-one men in all (not including the women and children). The following is a list of artillery and plunder.

120 iron cannons (six- to twenty-four-pounders)
50 Swivels
1 Howitzer
1 Cohorn
10 tons of musket balls
3 cart loads of flints

Crown Point Fort remains. *Photograph by the author.*

An eighteen-pounder cannon. *Courtesy of the National Park Service.*

30 new carriages
A considerable quantity of shells
A warehouse full of material for boat building
100 stands of small arms
10 casks of very indifferent powder
2 brass cannons
30 barrels of flour[21]

Following the surrender of Fort Ticonderoga, an impressed General Washington sent Colonel Henry Knox northward to bring the artillery from the two forts back to Boston, which was under siege from over one hundred British ships in Boston Harbor. By his own account, it took Knox three weeks in the stormy winter weather to travel the roughly 250 miles north from Boston to the forts at Ticonderoga and Crown Point. He arrived there on December 5. The fort's cannons were moved by oxcart over land and frozen water, right under the British command's nose, to Dorchester Heights, where they were mounted overlooking Boston Harbor. After losing cannons through the ice on lakes and other hardships—and with the assistance of General Phillip Schuyler—Knox arrived in Boston with fifty-nine cannons on January 24, 1776. They were subsequently used to fire on the British ships and soldiers, forcing the fleet to leave.[22]

In 1775, after a visit to the Continental Congress by Ethan Allen and Seth Warner, the Green Mountain Continental Army Rangers Militia (often referred to as Warner's Regiment) was established and ordered by Congress to be paid for by New York. The New York funding was done much to the chagrin of the Yorkers, as the Green Mountain Boys had a history of resisting their enforcement, terrorizing their lawmen and running them off what would become Vermont Territory. By that time, after Ethan's failed attempt at St. John, Quebec, and some other poorly planned and risky ventures, many of the Green Mountain Boys were beginning to lose faith in Ethan Allen's strategic planning capabilities. Ethan's bad decisions were starting to pile up.

Seth Warner was selected as the commander of the Continental Rangers, or Warner's Regiment, which was sometimes called the Green Mountain Boys. Warner's Regiment included many of the same personnel, but it was not to be confused with the pre-Revolution Green Mountain Boys. Incidentally, Seth Warner was reportedly over six feet tall, which was a foot taller than average back in the eighteenth century. He had nut-brown hair, blue eyes and was said to have a "manly manner." And Warner was no slouch in the charisma department.[23] (See chart 3.)

Henry Knox hauling cannons from Ticonderoga to Boston. *Courtesy of the National Archives.*

As another side note to Ebenezer's story, in 1775, Ethan Allen was captured and imprisoned for almost three years, during which time, Ebenezer was having a breakout military career. In that year, Allen was part of a company of men in Warner's Regiment that he had mustered from Poultney and Tinmouth, and he served in a miserable five-week scouting party in Canada.

As Vermonters know, the weather during the winter near the forty-fifth parallel can be most unforgiving. Silas Bingham, who was a member of Allen's company, recounted some of the November–December expedition. The highlights included marches into the wilderness and rowing bateaus up Lake Champlain and the Richelieu River. They were hunkered down for three days and four nights in swamps without shelter during incessant icy rains. As the weeks wore on, much colder weather came on, and the swamps and ponds froze over, food became scarce and they had a few skirmishes with the enemy. Finally, they intercepted some British provisions, so they were able to feast. Then they marched to and took possession of La Prairie. Bingham's Regiment supported the capture of St. Johns and prevented Governor Carleton's boats on the river from landing to relieve St. Johns. Finally, General Montgomery's forces arrived, and they captured Montreal.[24] The troops' enlistments were up in December, and some men came home from Canada, while others returned later, through deep snows, in order to obtain heavier winter clothing for the troops.

At that time, in January 1776, Thomas Paine, who had some Vermont connections, published *Common Sense*, a fifty-page pamphlet that advocated for American independence from Great Britain. If anyone had any doubts as to whether the ongoing struggle in the colonies was a civil war with the mother country or a war of independence, Paine helped change their beliefs. *Common Sense* sold 120,000 copies in its first few months of publication, and it quickly found its way throughout the Northeast and galvanized the Patriot cause. Congress recommended that the colonies form their own governments, and by July 4, they had adopted the Declaration of Independence in Philadelphia.[25]

During the Canadian expedition, Allen's commanding officer, Captain Potter, died of smallpox that December. Allen apparently returned to Vermont and attended Tinmouth's town meeting on March 12, 1776, where he was chosen as a selectman, a member of a committee to explore building a meetinghouse and a delegate to represent the town at conventions of the New Hampshire Grants. At that time, Allen was also granted a license to operate a public house in Tinmouth. The tavern would have served as a gathering place for community chatter, court trials and even religious services. We don't know if his tavern in Tinmouth ever came to fruition for lodging or as an event venue, as other things got in the way.[26]

By June 1776, Allen became a captain in Herrick's Rangers and a member of Gideon Brownson's detachment that was raised for the immediate defense of the Vermont frontiers. Allen was serving formally during the month of July 1776. Six years later, in 1782, Allen and others in Brownson's and others' companies were finally paid for that work by the State of Vermont.[27]

On July 24, 1776, the New Hampshire Grants met in a convention at Dorset, Vermont, and Captain Ebenezer Allen and Major Stephen Royce represented Tinmouth at that meeting. The delegates affirmed their support for the Declaration of Independence that was adopted at Philadelphia and made the same ultimate pledge that those delegates to the Second Continental Congress had made:

> *We, the subscribers, inhabitants of that district of land commonly called and known by the name of the New Hampshire Grants, do voluntarily and solemnly engage under all the ties held sacred amongst mankind at the*

> *risque of our lives and fortunes to defend, by arms, the United American*
> *States against the hostile attempts of the British fleets and armies, until the*
> *present unhappy controversy between the two countries shall be settled.*[28]

This document was signed by Ebenezer Allen, Seth Warner, Heman Allen, Thomas Chittenden, Ira Allen and forty-four other men. Thomas Braten from Clarendon refused to sign the statement. William Marsh decided it was time to fly his true colors, and after signing it, he fled to Canada, leaving his family in Dorset. His property was confiscated, and his return to the state was forbidden by an act that was passed on February 26, 1779; this act was enforced until November 8, 1780.[29]

Two months later, on September 25, 1776, Allen and the other delegates convened at Cephas Kent's tavern in Dorset and solemnly declared the New Hampshire Grants to be a "free and separate district." At the time, Captain Allen was thirty-three years old and had made a name for himself as a military officer and politician. His military skills, charismatic leadership ability and gutsy physical presence were useful assets when backing up the commitment for independence. At that time, patriotic Vermont settlers needed all the help they could get.

Let's summarize this important moment in history. The United States had approved the Declaration of Independence from Great Britain. Vermont had declared independence from New York and New Hampshire. The Revolutionary War had only just begun. Great Britain was not greatly impressed with the declarations one bit. Before the cannons arrived in Dorchester Heights from Forts Ticonderoga and Crown Point, there were 120 British ships in Boston Harbor and 400 in New York City. British general John Burgoyne had an army of roughly 6,000 troops in upstate New York, and there were plenty more British troops in Canada. Burgoyne also managed to win the help of thousands of Natives and Loyalists among the settlers (Tories).

BURGOYNE'S TERRORISM

In order to understand the climate of the 1770s in Vermont, we need to understand its political and military context. By 1777, British general John Burgoyne's terrorism campaign was continually threatening peaceful life in the Champlain Valley.

The majority of Burgoyne's well-equipped ten-thousand-man force were Natives from Canada, renegade Tories and German mercenaries. According to Wynn Underwood, Burgoyne believed the Natives lacked the subordination of his own troops, and he feared their bloodthirsty ferocity. He implored the Natives not to scalp wounded or dying men or to harm women and children, and he offered them rewards for returning with healthy prisoners instead of scalps.[30]

Burgoyne posted a proclamation on posters and through word of mouth in the Otter River Valley settlements, west of the Green Mountains; it warned of the force of the British armies and fleets and of the savagery and plundering of Burgoyne's Natives in the coming raids. Burgoyne also promised security and protection to all those who went about their work and did not evacuate their cattle or remove their corn and feedstock. He assured everyone that if they cooperated and obtained protection papers, they would be paid in full for feeding the British troops. Burgoyne's July "manifesto" read:

> *To the inhabitants of Castleton, of Hubberton, Rutland, Tinmouth, Pawlet, Wells, Granville, with the neighboring districts.…You are hereby directed to send from your several townships, deputations consisting of ten persons or more from each township, to meet Colonel Skene at Castleton, on Wednesday, July 15th, at ten in the morning, who will have instructions not only to give further encouragement to those who complied with the terms of my late manifesto, but also to communicate conditions upon which the persons and properties of the disobedient may yet be spared. This fail not to obey, under pain of military execution.*[31]

Once the proclamation had been issued, Burgoyne directed a campaign of raids, killings, kidnappings and destruction of settlements to back up his manifesto. Burgoyne believed the Natives had a reputation for being savages, and there is evidence he insisted on limiting killings and scalpings and pushed for the humane treatment of prisoners. Burgoyne promised the Natives gifts for humane treatment, including not molesting women. Unfortunately, the evidence shows, Burgoyne often did not come through with his rewards. And it is worth noting that Tory Loyalists were seldom held accountable for their brutality during the raids.[32]

Tory Sleeper Cells

The Tory infiltration of the settlements was very effective. According to Underwood, the Tories served as the British Fifth Column or Trojan Horse:

> *These men who had once lived as neighbors with the now-rebellious colonists knew every house, road, bypath and hideout in their native towns. They were some of the cleverest and most effective fighters in Burgoyne's army—pilfering, burning, alarming and undermining the morale of the Vermont settlers.*[33]

Since they appeared passive, the Loyalists could spy without being detected and could remain home on their farms while secretly selling produce or information about the rebel activities. Only about one-third of the colonists in America served in the militia, as their agrarian lives demanded time for work and families. Because of this, it was often difficult to ascertain a neighbor's sympathies. Since Loyalists knew the locations of the roads and paths, all of the town stores, provisions, munitions and so forth, it was easy for them to quickly and strategically target and destroy property and efficiently take prisoners.

Nearly all the Native raids showed signs of Tory leadership or association. Usually, these parties came directly into the Otter Valley from Burgoyne's headquarters on Lake Champlain or from Canada via the lake. The most conniving and best-led raids were accomplished by Tories who knew where, when and whom to strike. Sometimes they painted their faces to resemble the Native warriors to avoid being recognized in their own towns.[34]

In response to fears of the subversive Loyalist citizens who were hiding in plain sight, Tinmouth residents discussed ways to ensure that there weren't spies lurking and plotting among them. They voted to consider an oath of fidelity to the town as a way to identify sleeper cell terrorists in the town.

Prior to a special town meeting on April 14, 1777, Allen worked behind the scenes and circulated an oath of fidelity for people to consider. Some residents objected, saying the town hadn't decided on the need to pursue an oath. The town records indicate that Allen was correct; the town had indeed voted to consider an oath. Allen's suggested oath reads as follows:

> *You and each of you swear by the living God that you believe for yourselves that the king of Great Britain hath not any right of command or authority in or over the states of America and that you do not hold yourselves bound to*

*yield any allegiance or obedience to him within the same, and that you will,
to the utmost of your power, maintain and defend the freedom, independence
and privileges of the United States of America, against all open enemies, or
traitors, or conspirators whatsoever; so help you God.*[35]

THE ERA OF RAIDS

The concurrent fall of Fort Ticonderoga and Mount Independence in 1777
resulted in a lot of uncertainty. Settlers were already on edge from the raids
and Burgoyne's threats. Every man between the ages of sixteen and fifty
was required to join the fort militia, ready to fight; the only men who were
exempt were ministers and judges. The expected equipment included a
three-and-a-half-foot long rifle; a sword, cutlass, tomahawk or bayonet; a
cartouche-pouch or powder horn; a bullet pouch; a pound of gunpowder;
four pounds of bullets; and flints.[36] Of course, individuals like Ebenezer
Allen not only possessed the weaponry, but they knew how to use it well.
And whether they were on militia duty or not, they drilled on a regular basis.
And although many households had militiamen in the family, the men of
those houses weren't always present. And even well-prepared settlers faced
long odds during raids against a party of professional soldiers and warriors
who might catch them by surprise.

Word of mouth spread horror stories of the perils of living in Vermont
Territory. Shelburne was one of the many beauty spots in Vermont in the
1770s, and Moses Pierson had purchased a one-thousand-acre lot that gently
sloped down to a sandy beach by bonnie Lake Champlain. In 250 years, this
neck of the woods would be identified as prime lakefront real estate, with
rolling hillsides, jaw-dropping Green Mountain and Adirondack Mountain
views and a desirable microclimate.

But the tradeoff of living in northern New Hampshire Territory in 1770
was that, even in paradise, it was a very dangerous place to raise a family.
Pierson, his wife, Rachel, and their children moved to their Shelburne lot
and built a heavily fortified frontier house of hewn logs and a log barn.
The house had loopholes and removable blocks for the windows, as well
as a roof that could be "thrown off" in case of fire. The large family spent
the years between 1770 and 1776 improving the land and growing wheat
in the idyllic setting. They lived a peaceful, bucolic life for the most part.[37]
All kinds of bad things were happening around them in different parts of

the state, as New Hampshire land deeds were being ignored and challenged by New York governors and sheriffs. Attacks by British soldiers, Tories and Natives persisted, and the Piersons were bothered a few times by threatening intruders. The raids were traumatic, at the very least, and more often than not, they could be life-changing and life-threatening.

After hearing that a large raiding party was on the way, the family decided to move to the southern part of Vermont Territory in 1776. After waiting it out for a while and getting back a false sense of confidence, they returned in March 1778 with the intention of continuing to farm the land. Pierson was smart. He returned with Captain Thomas Sawyer, Lieutenant Barnabus Barnum, Corporal Joseph Williams and fourteen privates in the company to scout the territory, offer protection and serve another purpose. According to Brennan Gauthier, a Vermont archaeologist for the site, Sawyer was sent because he was a valuable commodity; he was to protect and thresh wheat stores that were being kept in one of Pierson's outbuildings.

The family was asleep in the wee hours of March 12, 1778. Out of the blue, an hour before daybreak, a sentry ran into the house, shouting to alert the Piersons that were under raid. The house was immediately under heavy attack by sixty Natives and British soldiers who were dressed as Natives. The house was set on fire several times during the gunfight. After they ran out of water, they used Mrs. Pierson's fresh batch of beer to extinguish the flames. But it was no laughing matter, Lieutenant Barnum, a British officer, a Native chief and several privates were killed in the battle. The Piersons' small girls and an infant, who were all lying in their beds, emerged unharmed, despite grapeshot hitting the headboards that were just above them. Two men who were passing through to buy wheat had stayed the night and were shot dead through the windows as they slept. Captain Sawyer's unit captured six British soldiers. The attackers retreated and dumped some of their dead and fatally wounded party members through a hole in the lake ice. The Piersons buried the chief and the British officer. The Americans were buried in coffins on the property.[38]

How did a family and small military detachment fight off sixty warriors and British soldiers? According to Gauthier, the attackers were hampered by their significant alcohol consumption; the mission failed, and a court-martial followed due to their poor performance.

Soon after the attack, the Pierson family packed up and headed to Clarendon and Rutland to live until the Revolution was over, leaving two older boys on the farm. The angry British command offered a reward for Moses Pierson, dead or alive. A while later, British soldiers returned to the farm, looking for Pierson. They burned down the buildings and took the boys (Ziba, age seventeen, and Uzal, age fifteen) to St. Johns, Quebec. They later escaped to safety and reunited to live with their family.[39]

Forts Pop up in the 1770s

The Pierson family's experience was echoed for families throughout the state, and the Piersons turned out to be lucky compared to others. Most early Vermont settlers didn't have the luxury of their own live-in military unit for protection. A handful of forts had been constructed during the French and Indian Wars in Vermont Territory, but most of them were on the southern border and, by then, were in disrepair.

In response to the perilous raids, beginning in the 1770s, the council of safety directed the construction of a series of new forts and blockhouses to protect settlers from raids and attacks, mostly at the latitude of the present Route 4. This order included forts in Pittsford, Castleton, Rutland, Newbury, Royalton, New Haven (Vergennes) and Bethel, to name a few.

Fort Mott, named for Deacon John Mott from Neshobe (Brandon), was built in the fall of 1777 on the east bank of Otter Creek, just south of the Neshobe line in Pittsford. The walls of the structure were composed of up to sixteen-inch-diameter hemlock logs that were driven into the ground like posts and pointed at the top. The west side of the fort walls extended down the bank of the creek so that soldiers could fetch water if the fort was under siege. The fort covered three-quarters of an acre of land and was square with a log house in the center to serve as a blockhouse. Ebenezer Allen was ordered to be in charge of the garrison in the spring of 1778, and records show that he was procuring provisions and supplies to support the detachment.

Fort Ranger at Rutland on Otter Creek, just east of Gookins Falls, was built by Captain Sawyer, who had defended the Shelburne Blockhouse Raid. The fort covered a roomy two square acres, included a two-story block house and housed a permanent garrison. Fort Warren, named in honor of Colonel Gideon Warren of Tinmouth, was built at Castleton in May 1779 by Captain John Spafford with thirty men from Tinmouth.[40] Around the same time, a blockhouse was built by Ethan Allen and his crew on Otter Creek. The small fortification in New Haven sat just above the falls on the east side of the river in what is now Vergennes to protect the settlers there from Yorkers.

Fort Vengeance sketch. *Courtesy of the Pittsford Historical Society.*

Ebenezer Allen was put in charge of the garrison, and he directed scouting parties there. These scouting parties produced some interesting skirmishes and dramas that will be revealed later.

In 1780, Fort Vengeance in Pittsford soon replaced Fort Mott, which had proved to be inadequate. All of the outposts were subjected to attacks, but the killings and kidnappings were all perpetrated on settlers who had ventured outside the safety of the stockades. Settlers were so vulnerable to Tory-Native raids that, as late as 1780, the council of safety proclaimed that settlers were not safe north of Pittsford, and the land north of Castleton and Pittsford was considered to be enemy territory without any military protection.

Fort Vengeance was located above Otter Creek and is now marked by a stone marker on the west side of Route 7. James Petersen, in *Otter Creek: The Indian Road*, describes the fort as a stockade that was built of hardwood tree trunks that were buried vertically five feet in the ground, with sharpened points that were sixteen to eighteen feet tall. The fort covered one square acre, which would have been roughly two hundred feet by two hundred feet. The fort also had a six-foot-high breastwork of logs and earth that was about six feet deep and backed up the pickets. Log sentinel boxes sat inside and above the corners, allowing soldiers to fire on attackers from every direction. The structure had east and west gates made of bulletproof double-oak

Fort Vengeance sketch. *Courtesy of the Pittsford Historical Society.*

planks, officers' and soldiers' barracks and a munitions magazine. The fort also had water wells and spring water inside the fort. Water also flowed from springs that were five hundred feet from the fort.

When the fort was completed, Major Ebenezer Allen was placed in command of a garrison of 150 men. Finally, Pittsford had a roomy, solid, overbuilt fort, with barracks for officers and enlisted men, towers at the corners, reinforcements, ammunition, weapons and 150 soldiers. What could possibly go wrong at the Pittsford Fort? An eyewitness named Henry Hall remembered the following anecdote, which describes the manner in which the fort received its final name.

Thirty-year-old Caleb Houghton, one of the soldiers in the garrison under Major Allen, left to visit a neighbor's house outside of the fort—he was unarmed. Houghton had bragged to the other men that he would never be taken alive and allow himself to be tortured or imprisoned. When he didn't return when expected, a party was sent out from the fort to look for him. They found his body about a half mile from the fort. He had been run through with a sword, shot with a gun so close that the wadding was in the wound and tomahawked.[41] Major Allen was apparently outraged and sent a detachment to search for the killers; they searched for several days, but to no avail. According to the men who were stationed at the fort, Allen gathered his men at the Pittsford Fort entrance and declared vengeance for the killing.

He smashed a bottle of rum against the studded double-plank oak gate and christened the new fort "Fort Vengeance."[42]

That same year, at its April 1780 meeting in Arlington, the board of war decided to design and erect another fort at Hubbardton. They discussed having Ebenezer Allen site and direct its construction. The board envisioned staffing a garrison of seventy-five men and completing it as soon as possible. There is no evidence that the Hubbardton Fort was ever built. Perhaps Allen had a few other priorities at that time.[43]

Evidence shows that Allen was the point man for siting, designing, acquiring the materials and manpower and building several forts. He was also responsible for setting up and commanding garrisons and directing scouting parties, with several bases going at the same time. With all of these fortifications going up, Allen must have been a very busy man. As we shall see in the next chapter, Allen had an invincible personality.

4

HERE, AS WE SIT!

As mentioned earlier, Loyalists, also known as Tories, were living next door to the Green Mountain Boys and their families, especially in the southernmost Vermont towns, near the Massachusetts border. That did not always go well. The Loyalists were sympathetic to the British cause, and in some cases, they acted as operatives for the British military. Mary Spafford, the widow of Tinmouth's Captain John Spafford, wrote:

> [Tories] *were more dreaded than the British themselves; they were constantly prowling about, which kept the whole northern frontier in a constant sate of excitement and alarm, committing depredations upon the inhabitants, which called forth all the energies of the people and kept the most active and influential men inhabitants of the frontier towns almost constantly in the field, and from July 1777 to the year 1781, my husband was constantly engaged in* [the] *army.*[44]

As conflicts continued to erupt between New York sheriffs who were attempting to enforce their own property deeds and New Hampshire Grant holders, tempers began to boil over, and Patriots started looking for solutions. The talk of and a vote for building a "gaol," or jail, in Manchester to hold Tories was passed on a vote at the 1776 convention in Dorset. Before long, the seizure of Loyalist properties became a tradition. How did this come about, and on whose authority was this done?

The Safety Committee of New Hampshire was one of many local organizations of Patriots that was formed, and they performed certain functions as a shadow government in the hands of American rebels. Safety committees were prevalent throughout the colonies. The local committees in the colonies and larger cities were able to usurp power from the British leadership and work in concert with committees on correspondence and committees on inspection (or committees on observation) to coordinate resistance.

The Vermont Constitution was written in Windsor on the same day that the Battle of Hubbardton took place, July 7, 1777. The constitution, which was based on the Pennsylvania Constitution, was adopted the following day. Before the general convention at Windsor was adjourned on July 8, 1777, a council of safety, later known as the Old Council of Safety and composed of thirteen men, was appointed to run the government until it could officially go into operation under the newly adopted constitution. The committee was directed to take custody of the estates of persons who were at odds with the American cause.[45]

Members of the Old Council became known as the governor and council and also acted as council of safety and board of war; it combined the power of the legislative, judicial and executive branches. The council met by agreement in Manchester on July 11, 1777, and it elected Colonel Thomas Chittenden as president and Ira Allen as secretary. This was a dramatic time for the new republic of Vermont, as there was a lot of violence, and the official government, which was an idea a bunch of guys made up based on their convictions, did not yet really exist.

At that time, Burgoyne's British army was putting a lot of pressure on the settlements, yet there were no funds in the Vermont treasury to pay for a militia. Ira Allen suggested that commissioners should generate funds by the sequestration, confiscation and sale of Tory property that had been distributed by New York. This property would be seized and sold at a public vendue or tax sale. This idea was quickly adopted and put into practice. Herrick's Rangers were soon created, and bounties were paid. A year later, the Vermont assembly made it official, and in addition, they passed acts for the punishment of high treason, treacherous conspiracies and other so-called atrocious crimes. This opened the door for an era of prosecutions, arrests and punishments before a formal judicial system had been created. In fact, Allen served as clerk at the ejectment trial of John McNeil in Tinmouth. McNeil had been one of town's founders and most prominent citizens prior to Burgoyne's invasion. He had been accused and convicted of being a Tory, and subsequently, all of his Tinmouth property was confiscated and sold.[46]

Allen served on the council of safety and carried out the orders that emanated from that group; the orders were designed to deny the Yorkers control of Vermont land. At that time, there were no checks and balances or oversight of the committees, so it would have been easy for the activities and missions to be unregulated, and it seemed like a matter of time before some of the hostile confrontations would go in a bad direction.

We can imagine that, since the committees were not regulated and danger prevailed on the frontier, it would have been possible for heavy-handed transgressions and abuses to take place against the Tories and New Yorkers who were carrying out the New York governor's orders. As we shall see, a lot of paramilitary missions emanated from the Vermont Council of Safety, and many of them were carried out by small, well-trained units that had served with the rangers. Allen was a key operative in these missions and would continue to be for the rest of the century. But Allen had other jobs, too. He served concurrently with Warner's (Continental) regiment and Herrick's (state militia) Rangers while they were on deployment throughout the Northeast and in Quebec, Canada.

AMERICAN INFANTRY RANGERS

The differences between the training and strategies of the British infantry and Herrick's Rangers were often great. The British were better dressed, with grenadiers wearing pointed bearskin hats and redcoat uniforms, and the American colonial army and state militias were much less consistent. But appearance was just the beginning. As Eliot Cohen pointed out in his book *Conquered into Liberty*, the European units were often composed of career warriors. In Europe, these men tended to be the poor and lower-class artisans, and military combat service was sometimes an alternative to prison. Soldiers were enlisted for a three-year term. Strict discipline was imposed, with punishments for breaking the rules including flogging and running the gauntlet. A gauntlet was a form of military punishment in which a soldier was forced to run between two rows of soldiers who attacked and struck him as he passed down the line. The two groups' strategies could be vastly different, too. European battlefields often consisted of more open spaces, unlike the thick wilderness settings of New England.

European linear tactics of the eighteenth century demanded that soldiers march in rank-and-file formation in the open combat battlefield area; they would march toward the enemy, often directed by commands signaled by fife and drums. Then, on command, within eighty yards of the enemy, the soldiers would fire into the rank-and-file mass of their bodies, hoping to hit someone. Then they would keep marching, all while reloading the muskets in fifteen seconds at best. On command, they would stop and fire again at closer range. When the soldiers in the front line were hit by return fire and felled, the ensuing lines would step over the bodies and continue marching and reloading. The marching, reloading and firing sequence would continue until the British were at point-blank range of their enemies. On command, they would charge with fixed bayonets and swords drawn for close-range fighting.[47]

By contrast, the American Patriots, or "rebels" as they were called by the British, who served in the ranger militias were more accustomed to woodland fighting. The citizen rangers tended to be intelligent, well-trained and were often excellent marksmen. They were familiar with the terrain in the New England territories, prepared for the changeable weather and acclimated to wilderness survival. They took defensive postures when they could and made each shot count. The rangers' deployment period often extended for weeks or months in duration, and then they would return home to their farms and families.

Light infantry woodland fighting. *Courtesy of the Ethan Allen Homestead Museum.*

Patriot, Commando and Emancipator

The warfare strategies used in the American light infantry were passed on from Rogers's Rangers company, which was a British light infantry unit that was created during the 1750s that fought during the Seven Years' War. That unit was adapted to reconnaissance missions and dense wilderness fighting scenarios, in which ambushes were common and conditions were less than ideal for linear tactics. These light infantry fighters had often developed what might be considered elite skills compared to the traditional army fighters. They tended to get well within musket ball range and fire at individuals instead of volleying with the hope of hitting someone in a mass of bodies. Rogers's Rangers' standing orders included:

Standing Orders Rogers' Rangers

1. *Don't forget nothing.*
2. *Have your musket clean as a whistle, hatchet scoured, sixty rounds powder and ball, and be ready to march at a minute's warning.*
3. *When you're on the march, act the way you would if you was sneaking up on a deer. See the enemy first.*
4. *Tell the truth about what you see and what you do. There is an army depending on us for correct information. You can lie all you please when you tell other folks about the rangers, but don't never lie to a ranger or officer.*
5. *Don't never take a chance you don't have to. When we're on the march, we march single file, far enough apart so one shot can't go through two men. If we strike swamps, or soft ground, we spread out a breast, so it's hard to track us.*
6. *When we march, we keep moving 'till dark, so as to give the enemy the least possible chance at us.*
7. *When we camp, half the party stays awake while the other half sleeps.*
8. *If we take prisoners, we keep 'em separate till we have had time to examine them, so they can't cook up a story between 'em.*
9. *Don't ever march home the same way. Take a different route so you won't be ambushed.*
10. *No matter whether we travel in big parties or little ones, each party has to keep a scout 20 yards ahead, 20 yards on each flank, and 20 yards in the rear so the main body can't be surprised and wiped out.*
11. *Every night, you'll be told where to meet if surrounded by a superior force.*
12. *Don't sit down to eat without posting sentries.*

13. Don't sleep beyond dawn. Dawn's when the French and Indians attack.

14. Don't cross a river by a regular ford.

15. If somebody's trailing you, make a circle, come back onto your own tracks, and ambush the folks that aim to ambush you.

16. Don't stand up when the enemy's coming against you. Kneel down, lie down, hide behind a tree.

17. Let the enemy come 'till he's almost close enough to touch, then let him have it and jump out and finish him up with your hatchet.[48]

Many of these rules would have been common sense to Ebenezer Allen, who grew up around Natives and spent most of his time in the great outdoors. We expect that these kinds of rules might have instilled some confidence and reassurance in the troops, some of whom might have been acquainted with the formality and vulnerability of British linear tactics, not to mention the prospect of fighting against hardened professional mercenary armies. Both armies would have endured dense wilderness missions, during which they were exposed to the harsh elements of nature and operated in unknown territory where ambushes were easily possible. While some historians argue that these woodland fighting techniques were factors in the success of the Americans in the Revolution, others, including Robert Grandchamp, assert that the British used woodland fighting techniques as well. Be that as it may, one thing is clear: much of Ebenezer Allen's incredible battlefield success was based on his exemplary woodland fighting leadership and techniques and his ability to stay healthy.

Military success and survival wasn't determined only by military strategy, skill and execution. It is well-documented that diseases were rampant throughout the eighteenth century, especially during the war. Zadock Thompson reported that, during the summers of 1776 and 1777, dysentery was universally prevalent in Vermont and New England. This disease produced great suffering and mortality in the American army, especially in the neighborhood of Lake Champlain, which was a main theater of the American Revolution.[49]

Of course, dysentery, which was characterized by fever and extreme diarrhea and dehydration, was caused by ingesting bacteria from human waste and contaminated food, among other things. One can imagine troops and warriors in bateaus and on ships, where human waste was routinely dumped in the lake, not far from the point where drinking water was collected at the other end of the boat. It would still be decades before the general public and even scientists would make the connection between microbes, which weren't even a concept yet, and diseases. With chamber pots and privies close to and potentially mixing with drinking water and a lack of basic hygiene practices, it is no wonder dysentery ran rampant.

Other diseases with significant mortality rates abounded as well. Oftentimes, men would be stationed in six-man tents, eating and sleeping in close quarters without social distancing for months at a time, under stressful, cold and wet conditions. Communicable diseases, including smallpox, influenza, pleurisy, typhus and scarlet fever, were easily spread in these scenarios. It has often been said that diseases killed more men than battlefield fighting during the Revolution and the War of 1812.

For those who stayed healthy, good clothing was essential. The regimental dress code was not always faithfully adhered to in the north country—or elsewhere in the colonies for that matter. In fact, one could argue that there was no dress code. Warner's Regiment dress uniforms included cocked black felt hats, green coats faced with red, buckskin waistcoats and breeches, coarse woolen stockings, heavy low shoes and checked and white shirts. In the field, they often wore rifle frocks. Not all of the troops were equipped with bayonets, and their arms were English or French muskets, although some carried American rifles.

Jerry Mullen of Warner's Regiment of reenactors, who has carefully researched the original regiment, says that only 60 percent of the soldiers in the regiment wore uniforms. Officers bought their own uniforms, and according to other sources, they usually carried swords and pistols. Mullen told the author of this book that it was unlikely the men in Herrick's Rangers wore uniforms, unless they had procured them from their work in Warner's Regiment. Since Allen was an officer in Warner's Regiment, it is likely he wore the green regimental uniform with pride while on duty.[50]

Green Warner's regiment uniforms. *Courtesy of the Ethan Allen Homestead Museum.*

Allen's particular blend of Native knowledge and military skills were an especially good match for the needs of a young Vermont republic. By all accounts, he was highly skilled, athletic, cool under fire, combat-savvy and perceptive. He was able to take orders and execute them, carry out special ops and defend the territory as needed. In fact, when we look at his personality, we see a man who was made for that moment in history. And unlike so many others, he somehow managed to get through it in one piece.

Allen's Unique Persona

What was Allen like as a person? His grandson Dr. Melvin Barnes Jr. of Grand Isle and Alburgh, Vermont, was twelve years old when Allen passed away, and he was well acquainted with him. He described Allen as a Calvinist fatalist and a Hamilton Federalist.

Calvinism was a common Protestant sect in colonial America during the 1700s. Its followers believed in predestination, the sovereignty of God, the supreme authority of the scriptures and the irresistibility of grace. Although there are no records of Allen's formal worship habits or service to the church, his behavior aligned with that of a fundamental Calvinist, id est, Protestant faith that was common at the time in the Puritan tradition.

Although no records show his direct involvement with the church, when we look at his stories, letters and quotations, we don't see cursing and other vernacular that was common parlance in the eighteenth century. When referring to the enemy in battle, he called them "rascals," even though we can imagine a number of other adjectives and nouns that might have seemed appropriate under those circumstances. One term he often used at the end of a sentence was "by the Jeez," which, of course, meant "by Jesus," but technically, he was not taking the Lord's name in vain. This might be comparable to a popular expression with today's Vermonters—"jeezum crow."

Allen's charmed legacy might have been enhanced by his faith in God, albeit without a record of strict church attendance. Even though Ebenezer did not have a church funeral, he deferred to God in his Tinmouth loyalty oath and, as we shall see, his emancipation statement. These two proclamations attest to God being a foundation of his core beliefs. Perhaps he was influenced by his cousin Ethan, who wrote the book *Reason, The Only Oracle of Man*. The book espoused a deist philosophy, which included a belief in a supernatural creator but one that didn't interfere in the lives of humans.

Political parties were not as well defined and certainly not as polarized as they are today. In fact, Vermont's first few governors didn't have strong party affiliations. The Federalist Party that Allen was said to embrace was the first political party in the United States, and it dominated during the final decade of the eighteenth century. The party was championed by Alexander Hamilton, and it led to the development of the U.S. Constitution and Bill of Rights. Federalists believed in a strong centralized national government with strong fiscal roots, for the good of all people.

Barnes described Allen as having a strong military manner and character, with black eyes, a large head, prominent features and a dark complexion. He had a deep chest, with long, stout upper limbs and short lower ones. He was also larger than average and was strong. Apparently, one of the pastimes of Ethan and Ebenezer and their lot was to pick up twenty-five-pound bags of salt in their teeth and toss them over their shoulders, competing for distance.

Barnes and others noted that Allen was very perceptive and benevolent. And at the same time, Barnes said, "His disposition left him imminently exposed to the designs of cunning and less scrupulous beings—to the views and artifices of the times."[51] Perhaps his big heart and generosity made him easily influenced by opportunities that were too good to be true.

After reading dozens of pages of land records that had been written and signed in Allen's cursive in the South Hero town clerk's office, it's possible to imagine a beefy, stalwart, weathered, forty-year-old Colonel Allen sitting across the wood table in his tavern. He would have to be somewhat extroverted with a reassuring command of the room. It's also notable that his handwriting improved over the course of ten years.

Allen's perceptiveness made him valuable as a frontiersman and a military man. But he wasn't a cunning, manipulative flimflam artist, like others were. From all accounts, Allen was a straight shooter in more ways than one. He was an action-oriented man with a lot of gumption. This might explain how he might have been hornswoggled by con artists along the way. After all, in the tavern business, he would have been exposed to every kind of nefarious character over the years. At any rate, Allen's personal qualities merited recognition and respect from his contemporaries. One has to wonder how he would regard some of our elected officials today.

Allen's combative personality yielded a man who was always ready to fight an enemy. As we shall see, he was a master of psychological warfare, and often, he created illusions that gave him the first jump and overwhelmed his adversaries. Some compared him to Myles Standish of the Plymouth Bay Colony. Standish was a skillful and brutal assassin and military commander, but he was also portrayed by Longfellow in a poem as a timid romantic. Unlike Standish, who was a widower, Allen fathered a large family, and they aged together. Even though he wasn't home much for a few years of the lives of his children, which was not uncommon in that era, there is no evidence of extracurricular dalliances, as was fashionable with some men. But Allen was quite prominent in his communities and the state.

As a child, Barnes listened to many hair-raising tales that were told by his grandfather, but he had no reason to believe they were exaggerated. An anecdote that speaks to then-Captain Allen's expectations for respect is the following episode about the aftermath of a battle and a traditional parade of the prisoners through a nearby town. For context, earlier in his short Ebenezer Allen biography, Barnes refers to Allen as "water and mountain," presumably in reference to the repose of his island home on Allen's Point, where the legendary former warrior was surrounded by spectacular water and mountain views.

In this story, Allen was accompanied by his lieutenant Isaac "Rifle" Clark, who was by Allen's side on many expeditions and battles, as we shall see. It was customary to parade the prisoners through town after a military victory. For example, the account of Thomas Mellen at the Battle of Bennington, which will be shared later, tells of the parade of captives who walked down the street in the town of Bennington after the American victory in that battle. It is not known if the next scene was a public parade in a town such as Bennington, but it is possible.

With today's hindsight, this story is dripping with stereotypes and will be offensive to some readers. It is a good example of what some would refer to today as casual, or everyday, racism. Rather than offering more social awareness or imposing my own interpretations and judgment on exactly what transpired, I will quote directly from Barnes's account of the event:

> *A great Indian chief, half-drunk, would come as near as water and mountain would let him, slapping those parts last seen going through a door, sustaining this person mounted on some stolen horse. After such repetition with impunity as the Indian thought, an end was put to the bravado by the captain, by allowing his lieutenant, Clark…to shoot the chief, which done, Capt. Allen barely told the superior the circumstances above, that the gun was discharged by his orders to subalterns.*[52]

In another example, Barnes recounted a corroborated story about Allen, who was eating with British officers in the mess at Quebec after the Revolutionary War had ended. This would have put Allen's age around forty or more. It is plausible that his reputation preceded him, as he was quite unpopular with British commanders. Apparently, Allen's combative

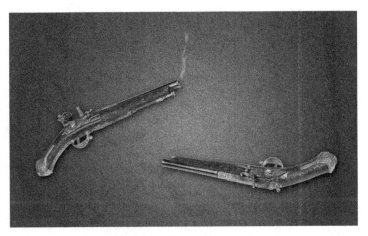

Pistols for a duel. *Courtesy of Alexander Lesnitsky from Pixabay.*

personality found a worthy opponent among at least one of his lunchmates. Allen had a way of abruptly exasperating and overwhelming his opponents. People who made the mistake of getting in a shoving match with him found that it went downhill quickly. This was one of those times. What was about to happen caught everyone by surprise.

Words were said. The trash-talking devolved to the point where one of the officers, who was sitting across the table from Allen, challenged him to a duel. Allen wholeheartedly agreed to the shootout. The other officer then asked when and where they should meet. Allen looked into his eyes with conviction and replied, "Here, as we now sit!" Drawing his pistol, he said, "I will take your pistol in my mouth, and you shall take mine in yours, and we will both fire at the word of command, by the Jeez!"[53]

There is no account of whether the British officer complied with Allen's brash retort or withdrew his challenge.

RAIDS AND ACTS OF WAR

long with the raid on the Pierson's farm in Shelburne, dozens of raids and attacks erupted in the New Hampshire–Vermont region during the 1770s. Carleton's raid down Otter Creek scorched, burned, kidnapped settlers and destroyed homes and infrastructure. The raids of Neshobe (Brandon) were also devastating to the early settlements and families. In some accounts, cabins and barns were built, destroyed, rebuilt and destroyed again.

In 1775, two men named Amos Brownson and John Chamberlain established homesteads in the area known as "the flats" in Williston. Not long afterward, a man and a child were killed in a Tory-Native raid at the Chamberlain farm. Allen marched a detachment to Williston to protect the Brownson and Chamberlain families and safely move them south, to Castleton and Rutland.[54]

The raid on Royalton by a combined British, Mohawk and Abenaki force on October 16, 1780, was one of the largest and last-recorded raids in Vermont. The harrowing ordeal was documented by a survivor named George Avery, a young man who was taken prisoner at his cabin in Royalton, Vermont, and forced to walk and paddle to St. Regis and then Montreal. There, he was indentured, first by a Mohawk family and then by a Jewish man. He lived for a year and a half before he was finally released in a prisoner exchange.

The British-led attack on Royalton was originally planned for Newbury, Vermont, but scouting reports had revealed a garrison there. A force of 265 Kahnawake Mohawk and Odanak Abenaki warriors was commanded by

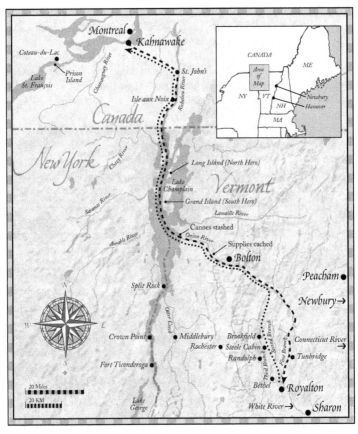

The route of the raiding party between Kahnawake and Royalton. *Courtesy of the Vermont Historical Society, 2010.*

Lieutenant Richard Houghton of His Majesty's Fifty-Third Regiment of Foot. The raiding party had marched from the Winooski River, camped out silently in Tunbridge the night before and attacked on Sunday morning. The attackers burned the village at Royalton and took 27 male prisoners; they then stripped them of clothing, bound them with neck halters and made them walk back to the Winooski River. The image above, from Neil Goodwin's *We Go as Captives: The Royalton Raid and the Shadow War on the Revolutionary Frontier*, depicts the route of the raiding party between Kahnawake and Royalton.

Avery was working outside near his cabin in Royalton on a Sunday morning in mid-October 1780. He was hungry and decided to head back to his cabin to get some breakfast. Little did he know that his life was about to take a turn for the worse. As he neared the clearing, he encountered several neighbors who were running for their lives. Their frantic message was that Natives were coming, and if he wanted to survive, he had better run. Avery was in the prime of his life, and although he took the alarm seriously, he figured he had time to duck into his cabin and grab a biscuit and his jacket for later. As soon as he stepped back outside the door, he came face to face with a Native.

The Native signaled Avery to go with him. Avery head-faked him and ran for the woods and down the riverbank behind the cabin, but before long, the Native caught up with him, whacked him smartly a couple of times on the leg with his tomahawk and gave him a choice: come with him or die there. Avery chose to live another day and followed his captor. By then, the cabin he had been living in with three other men was roaring in flames. In fact, he could see flames and smoke filling the sky from what appeared to be the entire settlement of Royalton. He, along with a group of other men from the town, were rounded up and herded together. After the group was given instructions, they were led away to begin a long, cold, hungry and painful ordeal that lasted several years. The prisoners were stripped nearly naked and walked barefoot, covered in dirty, flea-infested blankets, through snow and mud to the St. Regis Mohawk village in Canada. At night, the Natives tightly tied the prisoners by the waist to stakes that had been driven into the ground. In general, the prisoners were treated well, but in a couple of cases, captives were tomahawked, scalped and left behind for the pursuing rebels to find. Captives who were in uniform or otherwise known to be members of the American militia were administered more hostile treatment than those who were civilians.

At that time, there were forts in many of the Vermont towns, including Fort Defiance in Barnard and the Royalton Fort, which had been dismantled in order to build Fort Fortitude in Bethel, as it was thought to be more vulnerable than Royalton. Devastating attacks had recently occurred on Otter Creek and at Pittsford, and British-led attacks on civilians were happening as far west as the Ohio River Valley. The British saw raids as a strategy to cut off food supplies to the American militias as well as make the white settlers feel as demoralized and unwelcome as possible.

When threatened by a pursuing American force led by Colonel House from Hanover, the Natives released one of the prisoners, who had two sons that were also prisoners in the raid, to deliver a message to the rebels. The message was clear: if the raiding party was attacked, each of the prisoners would be killed. Avery said each hostage was tied to one Native, who was instructed to immediately kill their hostage if they were attacked. Once they reached the Winooski River, they boarded bateaus and dugout canoes and headed north on Lake Champlain under the protection of Carleton's fleet. They then paddled up the Richelieu River to the Mohawk village at St. Regis, Quebec. There, the prisoners were taunted by a steady stream of Loyalists who were fleeing their own hostile persecutions from Patriots in Vermont and New England.

Avery's story demonstrated that the British didn't have the ability to take responsibility for prisoners, so they gladly let the Natives enslave them as servants. According to historian Neil Goodwin, the kidnapping experience was repeated hundreds of times during the Revolution. Once in the village, Avery said there was a constant lack of food and clothing. He became sick from a leg infection and endured a nightmare of medical treatments and hospitalizations for weeks, and he finally wound up delirious and near death for days.

He survived by befriending a doctor in the hospital, and the doctor referred him to a businessman in a suburb. For the next year and a half, Avery did accounting work for the businessman, earning a shilling a day until he was released in June 1782 as a result of the Haldimand negotiations ceasefire, which was engineered by Ethan Allen. Avery finally made it back home to see his family, who had given up hope after hearing erroneously that he had been killed. After becoming reestablished, he settled down and married a woman in New Hampshire, where he lived a long and relatively happy life.[55]

In the towns without forts, settlers faced the constant threat of being attacked, taken prisoner and being killed. But Loyalists with British sentiments lived subversively among the Patriots in towns like Tinmouth, where Allen lived. The Loyalists were known as "protectioners" because they were receiving protection under British general John Burgoyne.

In one case, a Tinmouth man named Neri Cramton, who had been one of the original Green Mountain Boys with Allen at the capture of Ticonderoga, was abducted by British scouts. The only way Cramton would be released was if he submitted to the king and was taken under the protection of General Burgoyne. Knowing the other option was imprisonment and bondage—or worse—in Quebec, Cramton agreed to sign the papers. Then he returned home to Tinmouth. Later on, before the Battle of Bennington in August 1777, his family headed south to get out of harm's way in anticipation of

Frontier women in Vermont. *Courtesy of the Ethan Allen Homestead Museum.*

the battle and Burgoyne's predicted raiding parties. Cramton, however, took a detour to Bennington, fought as a Patriot with Herrick's Rangers and survived to return and live in Tinmouth. But other Tinmouth residents who were full-fledged Loyalist protectioners were not destined for the same fate.

THE IRISH AFFAIR

Five days after Burgoyne's manifesto warned Patriots of their impending doom, on July 15, 1777, Ebenezer Allen was appointed to the rank of captain in Colonel Samuel Herrick's Regiment of Vermont rangers. His payroll included sixty-two men. The council of safety anticipated raiding parties terrorizing the Patriots after the recent American surrender of Fort Ticonderoga. Most Tinmouth residents anticipated British-led attacks on their homes and families and left town to gather farther south in towns such as Arlington, Shaftsbury and Bennington or even Massachusetts, where it was thought to be safer. However, Loyalists stayed behind, since they had nothing to fear. Patriots had left their homes, provisions, crops and livestock behind, which were then vulnerable to attack and destruction.

In response to Burgoyne's threats and British-led raiding parties, American general Philip Schuyler ordered Colonel Seth Warner to send his men northward to round up cattle, livestock and wagons, as well as suspected Tories, and bring them back to Bennington. Allen and his Lieutenant Isaac Clark, who lived in nearby Middletown, just north of Tinmouth, were to take their company of rangers back to the Rutland-Dorset area. Following the initial roundup of livestock, Allen and his rangers were sent back into Rutland County on scouting missions by the council of safety.[56] Remember, the Vermont Council of Safety was an independent leadership and security group for the Republic of Vermont.

The council sent Captain Allen on a mission with a small tactical unit, including Tinmouth residents Major Phineas Clough, who would shortly become a Battle of Bennington survivor; seventy-one-year-old Tinmouth Green Mountain Boy John Train; and Allen's trusty lieutenant, Isaac "Rifle" Clark, to reconnoiter protectioners in the area. There was also word of a Tory camp in nearby East Clarendon that needed to be checked out. Two of the alleged Loyalist protectioners were brothers John and William Irish, who had built adjoining farms in Tinmouth. Their father, Jesse Clark, was also a Tory Loyalist living in Tinmouth. Although some historians say Allen's unit was nonmilitary, the Vermont militia records show that all four of these men were employed and being paid for their services in Herrick's Regiment, along with a number of others, from July to December 1777.[57]

Major Phineas Clough was an early farmer in Tinmouth and had also worked as a highway surveyor. He was said to be a hardworking and eccentric man. He didn't attend church services, but he was a member of the Congregational Society and was said to be very generous. On one occasion, the society discussed a measure that would cost a significant expenditure of money, and the frugal members quickly shot it down. Clough apparently stepped up and inspired the group and said that, although he wasn't a regular at church, he thought their property would be worthless if religion failed in the community. Thanks to Clough, the project prevailed, and religion was sustained in the town.[58]

Allen, who, by then, was an iconic leader in Tinmouth, had received information that the Irish brothers were indeed Loyalist Tories who had recently received protection papers from Burgoyne. Captain Allen ordered Clough to approach the Irish brothers on a ruse and tell them he wanted to join the Tories. John Irish told Clough to accompany him to his house, and he said that he would take him to the Tory camp but that Clough needed to go as a prisoner and sign papers first. Irish carried a raised tomahawk in his hand as they walked toward his house.[59]

Allen and his men covertly observed the encounter and took up concealed positions behind trees with loaded rifles from a few dozen yards away. Apparently, John Irish had gone to get papers for Clough to sign when Clough decided the jig was up and that it was a good time to make a run for it. Clough bolted out of the house and headed for the woods with Irish in pursuit. Irish stepped outside and warned Clough to stop; he said that he would shoot him if he ran.[60]

Irish aimed his gun at Clough. Allen, poised and ready, shot Irish in the left hand that was holding the rifle, and Irish dropped his gun. According to Melvin Barnes, Irish exclaimed, "Captain Allen, you have killed me!" At that point, Lieutenant Clark, aiming his rifle said, "No, he ha'n't, but I will." As Irish turned to face him, Clark shot Irish through the heart. According to Irish's wife, Rebecca, Irish turned toward the house, walked a few steps and then fell flat on his face, dead. After killing Irish, the party

Regimental troops firing rifles. *Courtesy of the Ethan Allen Homestead Museum.*

continued on to reconnoiter the Tory camp. Then they moved on to Arlington. If there was concern about the legitimacy of the shooting, Melvin Barnes commented, "Ample justification only required showing of the British 'listing orders,' to society at large, and if stained with blood, the better showing to us what the times were."[61]

John Train passed away peacefully later that same year in Tinmouth, and he left a son, Orange Train, who eventually served as a constable and a member of the Vermont legislature. Clough continued to work in the paramilitary capacity and didn't pass away until 1809. Isaac "Rifle" Clark reportedly

Eleventh Infantry insignia. *Public domain.*

carried out other well-executed orders similar to this one in his service with Allen. Clark was soon promoted to captain, and before too long, he married Governor Chittenden's daughter Hannah. He eventually became the distinguished Colonel Isaac Clark. Colonel Clark represented the towns of Ira and Castleton as an assemblyman, served as a Rutland County judge and, ultimately, commanded the Eleventh Infantry, which was stationed in a cantonment that he purchased during the War of 1812. Today, that cantonment is Battery Park, which sits high on a bluff with spectacular lake and mountain views in Burlington, Vermont. During his career, Clark's command was removed a couple of times, but he had it reinstated by the time of his honorable discharge.[62]

Rebecca Doty Irish, who had married Irish in her young teens, was twenty at the time of his death and claimed that she had witnessed her husband's killing. In 1842, sixty-five years after the event, Rebecca Doty Irish Stafford, who had subsequently married a man named Stafford, offered a different account of the killing of her first husband. She gave the account to C.H. Congdon, who published it in the *Rutland Herald* in 1855. It was also published in the *Town History and Map of Danby* in 1869. Rebecca Doty Irish Stafford would have been eighty-five years old at the time she told her story to Congdon in 1842.

According to Congdon, Stafford said that her husband, John Irish, was "Quaker in principle" and not a violent man. She claimed that he had broken down his gun and hidden it away in pieces after hearing "that all persons, irrespective of political sentiment, if found with arms, would be dealt with as enemies, and wishing to evade all trouble, he dismembered his fowling piece of its stock and lock."[63] Mrs. Stafford did admit that earlier in the month, on July 6, Irish did obtain protection papers from British general Burgoyne. She said Clough had sat in their kitchen doorway while the family had lunch and that Irish playfully laid on the bed with one of their children afterward. She also said that Irish ran out of the house after Clough, but she failed to state directly that he did or did not have a gun in his hand at that time of the shooting.

Stafford's contention was that Allen and his men were self-styled cowboys, and her husband was only three or four feet from the muzzles of their guns when they shot him. She also contended that, afterward, she had ascertained from others in the community that William Irish had a thirty-pound bounty on his head, and William Irish was most likely the man the posse was after, not her husband, John.

After the killing, Stafford claimed she promptly walked next door to her brother-in-law William Irish's house for help. William Irish, she said, had heard the shooting and was leaving town in a hurry—he told her she was on her own. Mrs. Irish, who had five children, two by her husband's prior marriage, hoped that neighbors might arrive and attend to the body of her husband, which was still lying on the ground outside of their home.

According to Stafford's story, after no one showed up to move the body, at dusk, she and her fourteen-year-old daughter and twelve-year-old son moved the two hundred–pound Irish onto a plank. The three of them slowly but surely slid him into the house. Stafford laid him out on the floor. John Irish was buried nearby the next day by two friends and Irish's father, Jesse. The next day, she walked seven miles through the woods to Danby with her three youngest children. The following November, John and Rebecca Irish's house was confiscated and sold to Judge Noble's father. Stafford then remarried and bore another six children by her new husband.[64]

Colonel Seth Warner, in his memoir, briefly recounted his version of the story, which corroborates that Irish was armed and chasing Clough with the intent to shoot him when Clark killed him. We don't know what evidence Warner's version of the story was based on, but as far as we know, Warner was not an eyewitness. In Warner's words, this story was promoted by the Tories as wanton murder by Lieutenant Clark. And Warner contended that, later on, when Rifle Clark became a public figure in civilian life, some of his political opponents revived the charge of murder against him for their own gain.[65]

We may never know which version of this story is closest to the truth. The first version was corroborated by Dr. Barnes and Judge Obadiah Noble.

Noble was described as having impeccable character. He served in public offices in Tinmouth for many years both before and after the event.

Stafford's official story was told many decades later through the veil of her Loyalist biases—not to mention her shock, pain and grief. By the time her story was told, another generation or two into the future, during the mid-1850s, the next generation may have forgotten the Tory terrorism of 1777 and that many Loyalists were aiding, abetting and committing raids. Furthermore, living on the frontier, it would not have been unusual to own more than one gun in the household, if not for protection, then for putting food on the table. Any hunter knows that you need a fowling piece or shotgun to hunt turkeys and other game birds and a rifle that shoots grapeshot to hunt mammals and big game. After all, settlers were constantly hunting and defending themselves from hostile people and animals, and guns were one of the essential tools of trade.

In 2009, a reenactment of the confrontation, shooting and mock trial was held by the Vermont Judicial Society in the old firehouse in Tinmouth. Townspeople acted out the roles of the characters, and prominent attorneys tried Ebenezer Allen and Rifle Clark before a jury of townspeople. Some believed it came down to the question: was this an act of war or an assassination? The verdict: Allen wasn't charged, and Rifle Clark was acquitted by a hung jury.[66]

At any rate, by 1777, according to the Vermont Council of Safety, Loyalists had proven themselves to be enemies of the state, and the council was actively holding "ejectment trials," sequestering, confiscating properties, arresting owners and punishing them. Scores of properties were confiscated during 1778–79, including lots that belonged to Ethan Allen's brother Levi. With all of the sympathy that is due to Rebecca Stafford and her family for enduring the traumatic killing of John Irish, Vermont was a hostile environment in which to be living as a Loyalist Tory. And given the prevalent British- and Tory-led attacks, which included burnings, kidnappings and killings, it's not surprising that Tories were being treated as hostile forces. After all, as we will see over and over again, Vermont was not yet a place with well-developed laws and a perfect judicial system. As we shall see shortly, Allen was about to become one of the most feared American rangers. Little did he know of the battles ahead.

6

"KILL THE GUNNER!"

A month after the Vermont Constitutional Convention took place in Windsor in August 1777, it was clear the British were planning an attack on Bennington's munitions and supplies. Families from the northern towns, such as Tinmouth, began to move south to safer areas, and Allen moved his family to a more protected territory in Bennington. Allen was called to serve with Captain Samuel Herrick's (Green Mountain) Rangers.

The Battle of Bennington, which occurred a few miles away in nearby Walloomsac, New York, was a big event that was months in the planning. Thousands of soldiers gathered from each side on the battlefield in mid-August. It was a war-defining battle for General John Burgoyne, who was facing New Hampshire militia general John Stark. The British military force included multiple units of professional Hessian and Brunswikker soldiers from Germany, British soldiers, Canadians, Loyalists and Natives. They were facing off against American Continental regiments and state militias from Massachusetts, New Hampshire and Vermont. General Stark spent months procuring powder, balls, rum, kettles and other necessities for the battle from anywhere they could be found.

Allen was scouting and fighting skirmishes with Herrick's Rangers, the well-trained, disciplined and hardy minuteman light infantry soldiers. These troops, especially Allen's unit, could move quickly, concealed in the backwoods, without a lot of provisions, and they could fight fiercely at a moment's notice. They were more like a special forces unit than a Continental army regiment, which tended to be slower-moving and often carried heavier supplies.

Warner's regiment formation. *Courtesy of the Ethan Allen Homestead Museum.*

On August 13, 1777, a few days before the Battle of Bennington, Allen and Lieutenant Clark and others who were out on a scouting mission were surprised at Sancoick, now North Hoosick, New York, by a party of Loyalists and Natives under British captain Justus Sherwood's command. Allen and

A John Stark statue at the
Bennington Battle Monument.
Photograph by the author.

Clark escaped back to Bennington, but five Americans were captured, as were a number of wagons, cattle and horses. Allen reported the advance of the Hessian, Tory and Native forces under Colonel Baum to General Stark at Walloomsac.[67]

After experiencing heavy rains for a day, trying to keep powder, provisions and men dry, the skies finally cleared on the morning of August 16. It was a sweltering, humid day, with the sun beating down mercilessly on the troops. This was the morning when American commander John Stark famously declared, "There are your enemies, the redcoats and the Tories. They are ours, or this night Molly Stark sleeps a widow." After the battle, Stark, who had had fought at the Battle of Bunker Hill, remembered it was "the hottest engagement [he had] ever witnessed, resembling a continual clap of thunder."[68]

The Heat of the Battle

The Battle of Bennington was remembered, many years later, by a ninety-two-year old battle veteran named Thomas Mullen from Wells River, Vermont. Mullen's first sentence of his account refutes the contention by many historians that Seth Warner and his men were late to the battle. Instead, based on his account, Stark may have saved Warner's unit from the initial engagements to rest them and use them as reinforcements later on. This was wise planning, since Warner's men were still fatigued from a long march, and by the time they came onto the battlefield, the enemy had been beaten up.

Mullen said, "Before the battle, as the armies were amassing, Stark and Warner rode up to reconnoiter the enemy, and were fired at, out of range, with cannons. They came galloping back, and Stark cried out to his men, 'Those rascals know that I am an officer; don't you see they honor me by firing at me with a big gun as a salute?'"[69] Apparently a cannon salute for the commander in chief and others was not uncommon during the Revolution.

After Mullen was engaged in heavy field combat for an hour or two on that blistering, humid day, he was sweating buckets and realized he hadn't drunk any water. He went looking for water and complained to an officer that he was dying of thirst. Mullen said the officer handed him his canteen, which was full of rum. Mullen said he drank plentifully and forgot his thirst. He went on to describe the combat. The enemy outflanked them and were closing in, and he said to a buddy that they had better look for cover, or they would be killed. His comrade responded that he wanted one more shot first. At that moment, a major rode up behind them on a black horse and shouted, "Fight on, boys; reinforcements close by." As he was speaking, a grapeshot went through his horse's head and knocked out some teeth. The horse bled, but the officer stayed in the saddle and spurred on to encourage others.

Within five minutes, Warner's men charged in to help. They came in behind them, and half of them attacked each flank and beat back the Germans who had been closing in. The unit took heart and stood their ground. Mullen's gun was too hot to hold, so he grabbed the musket of a dead Hessian. Right in front of him were the enemy cannons. Mullen shot twice at an officer on horseback who was waving his sword, ordering the gunners to fire the cannons. His horse fell. The officer cut the traces of a nearby artillery horse, mounted it and rode off. Afterward, Mullen heard that he had shot at Major Skene.

Soon, the Germans were losing men and ground, and they turned and ran, offering up or dropping their guns on the ground and kneeling before them. Unlike David McCulloch's accounts in *1776*, when Hessian soldiers in the Battle of Brooklyn bayonetted the surrendering Americans to make them suffer excruciating, lingering deaths, Mullen pushed the Hessians aside and ran over them, along with others in his unit. One wounded German lay flat on the ground, crying for water. Mullen grabbed his sword out of his scabbard and carried it in his teeth while he ran and fired. The Americans chased them until dark. Mullen reported that Colonel Johnston of Haverhill wanted to chase them all night, but General Stark overruled him, saying he didn't want to run the risk of spoiling a good day's work. He ordered a halt and a return to quarters. Mullen continued:

> *Warner rode near us. Someone, pointing to a dead man by the wayside, said to him, "Your brother is killed." "Is it Jesse?" asked Warner; and when the answer was yes, he jumped off his horse, stooped, and gazed in the dead man's face, and then rode away without saying a word....One Tory, with his left eye shot out, was led by me mounted on a horse who had also lost his left eye. It seems cruel now—it did not then.*[70]

That night, Mullen's company laid down and slept in a cornfield near where they had fought; each man had a hill of corn for a pillow. Mullen noted that when he woke the next morning, his body was so beat that he couldn't stand up until he had rolled around on the ground for a while. After breakfast, he watched others bury the dead. He saw thirteen Tories who had all been shot through the head, and they were all buried in one hole. Many historians note that, after battles, it was the civilians who buried the dead. The troops usually had orders or other more pressing matters to attend to.

A few yards from where he had fought, Mullen found a Captain McClary dead and stripped naked. He described scraping a hole with sticks and just covering him with soil. Many of the wounded had laid out all night. Mullen said, afterward, they marched to Bennington and saw the prisoners paraded. They were drawn into a long line: the British first and then the Germans, the Natives and, finally, the Tories.[71]

Plunder was common in warfare, and it was customary for the victors to take prizes with them. These prizes included weapons, hats, clothing, jewelry and more. But exactly what was fair game for plunder? During the heat of battle, some men were stealing personal property off living soldiers,

Seth Warner at the Bennington Monument. *Photograph by the author.*

whether they were injured or not. One doctor lost his instrument case. Others had watches stolen off their wrists.

General Stark was no rookie in battle, and he was aware of what the chaos of battle did to some men. He ordered all plundered items to be returned to one location after the battle so that the money and other effects could be divided equally among all of the winning soldiers at the battle. There were those who kept their spoils under threat of punishment and others who turned them in. In some cases, personal jewelry was returned to the original owner. It is possible that Captain McClary, who Mullen mentioned, may have been stripped of his clothes by plunderers who wanted an officer's uniform.[72]

Another account by a twenty-three-year-old named John Austin in the New Hampshire militia talked about approaching the rear of a British detachment through the dense woods. His unit sent several scouts out, and each time, they would bring little squads of Tories back, each with little pieces of white paper the size of a card stuck on their hats, identifying themselves as protectioners who were fighting for the British. The cards kept them safe, so they wouldn't be confused for rebel Americans and shot. Austin said, "We then advanced and fired. The main army in a moment fired also. We rushed on, drove the British detachment from their entrenchments and went in upon the main body."[73] Other accounts described some units of Americans inserting white papers in their caps so they could move in close to the German troops, who assumed they were Tories, and easily pick them off during the battle.[74]

Allen's Moments to Shine

Captain Allen's role on the battlefield that day was significant, and it was a preview for the ultimate outcome of the battle. He was known for being cool and decisive when facing extreme danger, and he was one of the best marksmen in the Continental army; he had faced Colonel Baum with his German troops from Burgoyne's army. Allen's unit had very little cover except for some field rocks and ledges. The lead grapeshot was flying everywhere. One account said that Allen, with a unit of thirty men and under the cover of the only boulders in the field, succeeded in a great slaughter of Colonel Baum's troops of Burgoyne's army, causing a temporary retreat.[75]

Obadiah Noble, Esq., repeated the story of Colonel Elisha Clark, Rifle Clark's brother, who was present. Colonel Clark was commanding an advanced guard, removing fencing between the woods and an open field with his division during the battle. Clark watched as Allen and his special unit overtook Clark's men and charged into the field. He said:

> *The British had a field piece placed upon an eminence, which very much disturbed the Vermont Militiamen. Gen. John Stark ordered Ebenezer Allen to take twenty sharpshooters from his company and go so near the cannon that they could shoot down the artillerymen until they would stop firing it. Allen, with his twenty men, moved on with great rapidity and overtook Clark….Just as Allen entered the field, there came a grapeshot from the field piece, which grazed his cheek and cut away a portion of his whisker. He put up his hand, rubbed his face, and said, "Them fellows shoot as careless as the devil." No more disconcerted than if a snowball had been thrown, he rushed on, made the attack upon the artillerymen, and…in a very short time, all that were not killed or wounded, fled and left the gun. Allen spiked it and returned to the main body of the army.*[76]

Another account that was written in a pension affidavit by John Knight, a soldier who had served in Allen's unit, said, during the battle, they faced two cannons, and they killed three gunners in one shot. Once they captured the

Battle of Bennington. *Courtesy of the National Archives.*

cannons, they turned them against the enemy and killed Colonel Baum and Colonel Fester with the Tories. Perhaps both accounts are true; they may refer to different scenes or the same one.[77]

We can only imagine what the British gunner crew that faced Allen's squad were thinking. Amid the continual clap of thunder, three men would drop dead simultaneously. Each remaining man on the crew realized if they were lucky, they might have fifteen seconds of reloading time to clear out of there before a sharpshooter would fire the next musket ball that would likely hit him.

Twenty-two-year-old Private William Boutelle from Leominster was in a unit of the Worcester, Massachusetts militia, and General Stark had kept his unit, as well as a few others, out of the action in first engagements of the battle. Finally, Boutelle's unit was ordered to march into a low field. Before long, they suddenly realized they were in plain view and almost surrounded by enemy soldiers, and since they were within about one hundred yards of the enemy, they were well within the range of their two cannons. Suddenly, all hell broke loose. As Boutelle said:

> The enemy immediately poured in upon us cannon ball, grapeshot and leaden balls as thick as hail, whizzing about our ears; it was a critical moment with us—our major [John Rand] had his horse shot through the head and cut off the head stall of its bridle and a cannon ball cut a lane though his horse's mane.[78]

Rand quickly ordered the unit to retreat, leaving one man dead on the field. They backed off about two hundred yards, where they would be sheltered from the blazing enemy fire. Then they waited for reinforcements for what seemed like a long time. All the while, they prayed the enemy wouldn't charge and advance on them. Before too long, General Stark rode up with considerable reinforcements and cannons that Allen's unit had captured from the earlier engagement. When General Stark arrived at the edge of the field, he cried out, "Fire on, my brave men, we shall soon have them." Stark's men fired off the cannons, which were devastating to the enemy. The Americans cheered and charged forward. The enemy fled in confusion and chaos, leaving their cannons with their horses dead in their harnesses. As the American Patriots advanced to the enemy position, the ground was littered with dead bodies, and the Patriots continued the chase.[79]

The Battle of Bennington victory was of enormous significance. The Patriots proved that they could beat professional soldiers. By the end of the Battle of Bennington, Stark's American army of 2,000 Patriots had killed, captured or wounded 1,000 of the 1,400 British forces. The American losses were put at 200. The Americans also captured four British cannons, many muskets and rifles and denied the British much-needed provisions. They undermined Mohawk support for Britain, and to many historians, this victory led to Burgoyne's eventual surrender. The battle changed morale across New England as word spread of the victory. It was the first of several victories that led to Burgoyne's surrender at Saratoga later that year.

After winning the Battle of Bennington, New England had a reputation to be proud of. On August 20, 1777, referring to the battle, British general John Burgoyne wrote:

> *Wherever the king's forces point, militia to the amount of three or four thousand assemble in twenty-four hours; they bring with them their subsistence, etc., and the alarm over, they return to their farms. The Hampshire Grants in particular, a country unpeopled and almost unknown in the last war, now abounds in the most active and most rebellious race of the continent and hangs like a gathering storm on my left.*[80]

What fate awaited the captured prisoners of the Battle of Bennington? General Stark had taken five hundred Hessians and British regulars and thirty-seven Tories who were all put into the Bennington Meeting House. The Tories were eventually removed, yoked together with ropes around their necks and marched off to the Northampton Jail. But the majority of the prisoners were left to be guarded. Many were eventually shipped off to Albany, New York.[81]

After the Battle of Bennington, the Americans celebrated the victory, but the soldiers and the families of the dead and wounded American soldiers faced grief and loss. Burgoyne's army was still in Upstate New York, although demoralized and weaker both physically and psychologically. Tories were still hanging around, and Vermont was not a safe place to be. American leaders came up with a new strategy to fight Burgoyne and his army.

The Pawlet Expedition

After fighting in the Battle of Bennington, Herrick's Rangers had a couple weeks of reconnoitering the area of Rutland County and Otter Creek. In the meantime, General Washington suffered an enormous loss on September 11 at the Battle of Brandywine in Pennsylvania; it was a battle with combined forces of almost thirty thousand men. An eleven-hour battle ensued, and American troops were able to retreat without complete annihilation. That loss led to the British takeover of Philadelphia two weeks later.

In Vermont, several New England state regiments were called together from the vicinity of southern Vermont for a new mission in Pawlet. Allen served in the three-month Pawlet expedition force, again with Herrick's Rangers, along with two thousand other soldiers from Massachusetts, New Hampshire and Maine. Pawlet was a strategic location to divide, divert and harass Burgoyne's armies and keep them under control. At that time, in 1777, the wagon road went only as far north as Pawlet, so any troop movement by either the American Patriots or the British army had to be done on foot or by water with limited supplies. During the Pawlet expedition, none of the troops had tents, and they slept under the stars in lean-tos, barns or other shelters if they could find them. Their presence must have had an impact on the tiny town bordering New York.[82]

Feeding a couple thousand men for several months was no small task. The food rations in the colonial regiments varied with what was available in the colonies, and the Pawlet mission was well-documented. The rations included plenty of beef on the hoof and flour from local farms. There was no way to transport live animals for slaughter, since the roads traveling north were nonexistent, but as long as the troops were stationary, there was plenty of food.

Each unit had a kettle, which was often the only cooking utensil they were provided. Bread and fire cakes could be cooked in the kettles, and the rations also included pork, peas and chocolate. It was believed that boiling beef was healthier than cooking it in other ways. Stews were a favorite, with local vegetables available. Vegetables were referred to as "sauce" during that era. We cannot imagine that the fat was skimmed off the soups or stews, and the belief about boiled beef is mystifying. Germ theory was still half a century away. Maybe it was believed that boiling ensured that the meat was safer, whereas rare meat, cooked on a fire and possibly in the dark, was associated with illness. When possible, food was bought by the commissary from the local farmers. Although rum was ordinarily a ration, there is no record of rum being rationed at Bennington or Pawlet.[83]

Fire cakes were a staple of the Revolutionary War soldiers, since they were hard enough to not fall apart in a knapsack and could keep for days or weeks. They consisted of biscuits made from flour, water and salt. After mixing, they were shaped into biscuits and either cooked right on the coals or ashes in a fire or in a kettle. In order to preserve them for later, they would be cooked a little longer until they became hard and crusty. Although this may not sound all that appealing, after several days with no food and limited water, fire cakes would be very welcome. The Pawlet expedition menu was not all that different from that of the Continental regiments.[84]

In general, the Continental army's rations typically included a variety of food and beverages depending on what was available in different regions of the colonies. In 1775, the Massachusetts Provincial Council and Congress had set the daily allowance, or ration, for American troops:

> *One pound of bread; half a pound of beef and half a pound of pork; and if pork cannot be had, one pound and a quarter of beef; and one day in seven, they shall have one pound and one-quarter of salt fish, instead of one day's allowance of meat; one pint of milk, or if milk cannot be had, one gill* [half a cup] *of rice; one quart of good spruce or malt beer; one gill of peas or beans, or other sauce equivalent; six ounces of good butter per week; one pound of good common soap for six men per week; half a pint of vinegar per week per man, if it can be had.*[85]

At Valley Forge, in the spring of 1778, General Washington ordered that, every day, the twelve thousand men encamped there, were each to receive:

- *One and a half pounds of flour or bread.*
- *One pound of beef or fish.*
- *Three-quarters of a pound of pork.*
- *One gill of whiskey or spirit.*
  or
- *One and a half pounds of flour.*
- *One-half pound or pork or bacon.*
- *One-half pint of peas or beans.*
- *One gill of whiskey or spirits, as or when they were available.*[86]

Generally, when in camp, the troops sheltered in tents, except when in cold areas during the winter. Six soldiers shared a tent or "hut" as they were called. Similar to navy practice, six men created a "mess," which was an eating unit that received the rations for those six men, and then they cooked the food themselves. When soldiers had families on campaign with them, the women companions were also included in the rations, and usually, the women served as cooks for their mess.

We know from captured personal accounts of British fortifications, British army rations were no better and, in some cases, much worse. The 1775 Fort Ticonderoga spoils included pork, peas, beans and flour. British diaries show that some British soldiers complained about subsisting for months on nothing but salted pork and bread.

By the end of the Revolution, some doctors believed that close accommodations increased the risk of some diseases. Smallpox, dysentery and pneumonia ran rampant in the eighteenth century, and of course, all were highly contagious diseases. The Pawlet camp was a convenient staging area for attacks on Burgoyne's garrisons, and Herrick's Rangers were about to get very active.

ALLEN'S BRAZEN COMMANDO ATTACK ON MOUNT DEFIANCE

In September 1777, Allen was appointed to the rank of major in Herrick's Rangers and served with Colonel John Brown on a mission to sweep the British from the north end of Lake George. Brown's detachment engaged in skirmishes at Lake George and attempted to destroy British ammunition and weapons on Diamond Island. They did destroy some outposts and supply lines but also lost some men. Allen subsequently was ordered to capture Mount Defiance near Fort Ticonderoga. It was there that Allen's commando skills really paid off.

At the time, the fort was occupied by a British force, with additional protection from nearby Mount Defiance. Scouts in the area had reported seeing British soldiers hauling two brass eighteen-pounder cannons up the steep road to the summit of Mount Defiance; they were placed there to defend the hill, lake and the fort below. Mount Defiance, then known as Sugarloaf, is an 850-foot-high hill. As a result of erosion, the mountain has craggy sides near the summit and is steep all the way around. It was nothing like the improved hiking trails we use on similar hills today. Attacking a guarded, steep, 850-foot-tall mountain that was occupied by two hundred men on foot, without artillery or air support, might seem like a high-casualty mission at best. The only access to the summit was a cleared path that wound its way up to the plateau at the top. The path would be easily guarded and defended, and it was the only practical access. Colonel Brown knew that if he wanted to have any chance of taking Fort

Ticonderoga, he would first need to take the mountain to eliminate the defensive position above the fort.

Colonel Brown must have known what he was doing when he ordered Allen to attack the mountain. It was a formidable and dangerous assignment, facing hardened British soldiers with swords, bayonets, rifles and devastating cannon fire if they failed. On September 18, 1777, under the darkness of night and with Lieutenant Isaac Clark, Allen led forty men to scale and scamper up the cliffs of the mountain. As usual, they used owl hoots to signal as they moved up the hill in the darkness. They stayed on the opposite side of the road to avoid detection, and the final ascent took place on a vertical rock face. Allen had one of his men stoop down so he and the rest of his men could climb up onto their shoulders and make the summit. Only eight men could be concealed without exposing the unit to the British. Once they were on the summit, Allen charged with "a hideous yell," and in Allen's own account, he said his men "came after him like a swarm of hornets."[87]

The rangers fired on the British troops. The panicked enemies who were not killed or injured quickly fled down the path, except for one soldier who lit a match to fire the cannon at Allen's men. Allen cried, "Kill the gunner," while firing at him with his musket. The gunner turned and fled with the rest of his unit.[88] In Barnes's version of events, Allen bellowed, in a stentorian voice, "Shoot them rascals!" Whatever was said, we can gather that it did the trick, as the British quickly vanished from the summit. Captain Allen had never fired an eighteen-pounder cannon before, but he fired several shots before quitting the summit. According to Ira Allen, Captain Allen killed one man and drove a ship from its moorings on the lake below the fort. Before Allen descended the mountain, he proclaimed himself commandant of Mount Defiance. Fortunately, there were no casualties in his ranger unit.

The entire British garrison was captured by Major Benjamin Wait and his men at the bottom of the mountain. After a distinguished career in the war, Wait served as a high sheriff in Vermont and became the founder of the town of Waitsfield. But that's another story.[89]

With Allen's charisma, who wouldn't have followed him up the mountain? What choice did the British soldiers have after awaking to blood-curdling war whoops, musket fire and a spray of grapeshot? The surprised British likely left their belongings at the summit, only to be captured and herded as prisoners in their pajamas, facing all the joys that came with confinement for the foreseeable future.

After pulling off one of the greatest excursions in his career, Allen was complimented by the Vermont Council of Safety for his "spirited conduct"

Vermont Militia reenactors firing rifles. *Courtesy of the Ethan Allen Homestead Museum.*

in action. To some historians, Allen's capture of Mount Defiance was his greatest achievement. The story would be told and told again, and Ebenezer Allen would become a household name, the hero of Mount Defiance, not only in the colonial and state militias, but also in taverns all over the Northeast and in the minds of the troops of the northern British army.

After the capture of Mount Defiance, one thousand American troops, under the command of Colonel Brown, surrounded Fort Ticonderoga. The British appeared to be well-defended inside the fort, but Brown knew that back in 1758, four thousand French defenders had repelled an attack by sixteen thousand British troops on the same turf. Brown had been ordered to not proceed with an attack if it meant any significant losses of American troops. During the standoff, Brown spent several days demanding and redemanding a surrender and offering prisoner exchanges in a battle of nerves.

True to his daring personality, the demigod Allen decided he would go on a scouting expedition out in the open to see what he could learn about the size and condition of General Watson Powell's force. Allen tied a piece of white cloth onto the end of his musket and strolled alone toward the fort.

He was able to ascertain that the British group was not a large force and that they were not prepared for intense combat.

Two letters from German officers tell slightly different versions of the story. One account says Allen approached with a white cloth on a stick and with a letter demanding a surrender.[90] But as we shall see from British general Powell's comments, Allen's foray was not well received. Nonetheless, even though the Americans realized they probably vastly outnumbered the British inside the fort, they lacked the fortitude to attack. One cannot help but wonder what might have happened if Allen had been in charge instead of Colonel Brown.

Following that episode, on October 30, an obviously miffed General Powell communicated with Colonel Herrick of the Vermont rangers:

> *I was very much surprised three days ago, when informed that Capt. Ebenezer Allen, under sanction of a white flag, without a drum, or even a letter from you, presumed to approach this garrison; but imputing it to ignorance of the rules of war, I suffered him to return....I inform you that I will further look upon such persons as spies...and to treat them accordingly.*[91]

Powell was referring to the custom of using a drum to communicate official protocol during a military engagement. Fifes and drums were widely used for communication and to signal alarm on both sides. Allen was not ignorant of the rules of war, but he was curious enough to see what would happen. He apparently got under Powell's skin.

Brown had no way of knowing the difficult conditions inside the fort, but surely, Powell must have been aware. On September 26, a German officer under British command, Major Friedrich Wilhelm von Hille, wrote:

> *On account of the many detachments and sick men, the regiment was very weak so that the comp. at times had no more than some 20 men at the alarm places and that each man had to be positioned at more than double distance from the other. The situation of the supplies was deplorable since we were still given nothing but wheat bread and salted pork. On days of fighting, Brig. Powell let every man have 1/8 quart of rum as a large bonus; fresh meat, vegetables and rice would have been better....A few days ago, a batteaux arrived from Canada with potatoes for which one had to pay 6 sch [shillings] per himten [2/3 bushel] and another with 30 head of lean rams, each of which was sold for 7 piaster [about 8 1/2 talers].*

You could not get wine at all these days. You could conclude from this how it stood here with foodstuffs in general.[92]

Von Hille's letter alludes to the deplorable diet and food rations inside the fort. And although, to some, offering a bonus gill of rum may have seemed like a good idea at the time, as Von Hille noted, even the soldiers would have appreciated fresh meat, peas and rice in place of a couple of shots of rum.

Brown's campaign was generally thought of as a failure, since the rangers were not able to score significant victories at Lake George and capture Fort Ticonderoga. But in fact, Brown's expedition had a significant impact on the British. Historian Edward Hoyt noted that Brown's surprise missions captured six British outposts, including Lake George Landing and Mount Defiance. During this mission, he released 118 American prisoners and captured over 330 enemy soldiers. He took possession of two hundred boats, including seventeen gunboats and one armed sloop. He seized numerous carriages, heads of cattle, horses, cannons, arms and ammunition. He also captured a considerable amount of plundered goods near the fort, including clothing, rum and other stores, and sent more than five ox team loads of plundered items to Pawlet and, later, Bennington by the end of September.[93]

A few weeks later, military records show that Allen's unit was a part of the company at the north end of Saratoga that prevented Burgoyne's retreat to Canada during Burgoyne's surrender on October 17, 1777.[94] And after that, Allen commanded another military conquest, and because of his ethics, the victory turned out to be a ground-breaking social activism landmark.

Not Right in the Sight of God

British general John Burgoyne had surrendered his army in Saratoga, New York, in October 1777. Afterward, Allen's company had returned to their base camp in Pawlet, Vermont. The surrender led to British troops departing from their installations, including Fort Ticonderoga, and retreating toward the safety of Canada. At Pawlet, Allen received orders to round up the rearguard of the Ticonderoga garrison, who were making their way up the New York side of Lake Champlain.

Allen headed north with a company of fifty rangers in the crisp fall air and crossed the cold lake at the narrows. After marching about eighty miles and camping out for a couple of nights, Allen's company caught up with the rearguard near the Bouquet River, north of Essex, New York. Allen's company surrounded the British unit disguised as Natives. They staged a scene where the woods appeared to be full of Herrick's Rangers, who were known to the British as "White Indians." Apparently, Tories and British soldiers weren't the only ones who were dressing up as Native people. The rangers' notoriety for their stealth and surprise had become legendary throughout the Northeast, and their presence struck panic in the hearts of those British troops.[95]

The British rearguard troops were sufficiently caught off guard, and they quickly surrendered to the rangers. As Allen would later recall, the captured possessions included three boats, one hundred horses, four cows, a number of goats, twelve yoke of oxen, some wagons and anything that wasn't nailed down from Fort Ticonderoga and Crown Point.[96] The prisoners were marched back to Pawlet and Bennington. Among the British property was a British officer's enslaved Black woman named Dinah Mattis and her two-month-old infant child, Nancy; they were stowed in a wagon.

Once at camp, Allen reacted to the capture of Mattis by first talking with his men about what he was going to do. Finding their agreement, he took leave of the detachment under his command to handwrite a certificate of emancipation and deliver it to the Bennington town clerk's office, setting Mattis and her child free. His logic was that, based on the determinations of the Continental Congress, all prizes belong to the captors, and he was of the mind that that it was not right to keep enslaved people. He believed his statement would set Mattis and her child free and keep them from further harm. Allen's emancipation statement, verbatim, reads:

Head Quarters Pollet
28th of November 1777.

To Whom in may concern know ye,
Whereas Dinah Mattis, a negro woman and her child of two months old was taken prisoner on Lake Champlain with the British troops… by a scout under my command, and according to a resolve passed by the honorable Continental Congress. That all prizes belong to the captivators thereof—therefore, she and her child become the just property of the captivators thereof—I being conscientious that it is not right in the sight of God to keep slaves—I therefore obtain leave of detachment under my command to give her and her child their freedom—I do therefore give the said Dinah Mattis and Nancy her child their freedom to pass and repass any where [sic] *through the United States of America with her behaving as becometh, and no trade and no traffic for herself and child as though she was born free, without being molested by any person or persons. In witness whereunto I have set my hand or subscribed my name. Evenezer Allen, Capt.*[97]

This certificate was recorded by the Bennington town clerk.

In Ebenezer's time, too often, the status quo was to accept enslavement as a norm and not challenge it. Allen's emancipation proclamation was powerfully significant, as he overcame the inertia of inaction, publicly took action and, no doubt, inspired others to take a stand as well.

Ebenezer Allen's emancipation of Dinah Mattis. *Courtesy of the Bennington town clerk's office.*

Contemporary writer Isabel Wilkerson describes radical empathy in her book *Caste*. Radical empathy opens one's spirit to the pain of another as they perceive it. When one person from a dominant caste sees another who suffers from oppression, the price of privilege is the moral duty to act.

An Ebenezer Allen mural painted by Stephen Belaski of Bellows Falls, Vermont. *Photograph courtesy of Ruxana's Home Interiors and the Works Progress Administration.*

VERMONT ABOLITION?

A few months before, in July 1777, Allen represented Tinmouth at the convention in Windsor, where the Vermont constitution was written. At that convention, Vermont acknowledged its independence from New York and New Hampshire and also made enslavement illegal. However, the constitution made the bondage of adults illegal. But technically, it was legal to own enslaved children. The abolition of adult enslavement went into effect, though largely unenforced, the following year, 1778.[98]

Almost ten years later, in 1786, the Vermont assembly rewrote the constitution, which included the following statement:

A DECLARATION OF THE RIGHTS OF THE INHABITANTS OF THE STATE OF VERMONT

THAT all men are born equally free and independent, and have certain natural, inherent and unalienable rights; amongst which are, the enjoying and defending life and liberty—acquiring, possessing and protecting property—and pursuing and obtaining happiness and safety. Therefore, no male person, born in this country, or brought from over sea, ought to be holden by law to serve any person, as a servant, slave, or apprentice, after he arrives to the age of twenty-one years; nor female, in like manner, after she arrives to the age of eighteen years; unless they are bound by their own consent after they arrive to such age; or bound by law for the payment of debts, damages, fines, costs, or the like.[99]

Notice that owning children was still perfectly legal and that the age of manumission was twenty-one for males and eighteen for females, which allowed for the ownership of minors. This also offered a loophole that permitted slavery if they were supposedly bound by their own consent. Also note that the statement used the word *ought* and not the more legally binding *shall*. Apparently, by 1786, the Vermont legislature had decided that trading enslaved people should be illegal, based on new legislation.

The Sale and Transportation Act of 1786 set a penalty of one hundred pounds for anyone who was convicted of conveying "any subject out of this state [Vermont] with intent to hold or sell such person as a slave." It was not until 1806 that Vermont legislators enforced a ban on out-of-state sales with an "Act to Prevent Kidnapping," which established tougher penalties for

The Old Constitution House, where the Vermont Constitution was written and adopted in July 1777. *Courtesy of Pernelle Voyage.*

trading enslaved people, among them, public whipping and imprisonment for up to seven years.[100]

Despite the good intentions of the legislature, the anecdotal evidence shows that enslaved people were openly owned in Vermont as late as the mid-1800s. A sobering example of this is Ethan Allen's daughter Lucy Caroline Hitchcock, and her husband, Samuel Hitchcock, who brought enslaved people from South Carolina with them to live in Burlington in 1835, fifty-eight years after the Vermont Constitution had abolished slavery.[101]

THE MORAL MANUMISSION

The plundered goods from military operations included food, alcohol, weapons, jewelry, clothing, hats and other souvenirs. But in many cases, there was a custom of respect between opposing officers that led to the protection of personal property. Even during instances of plunder, personal items and property were sometimes returned or compensated. In fact, after the capture of Fort Ticonderoga, in which Ethan Allen's men drank every last drop of the fort's ninety gallons of Captain Delaplace's finest Jamaican rum, Connecticut apparently reimbursed him for it.[102] But in this case, two captured enslaved people were neither plundered nor returned.

It is worth noting that, in a 2014 *Seven Days* interview, University of Vermont (UVM) professor Harvey Amani Whitfield praised Allen's decision to free Mattis, calling it "glowing significance" of his ethical decision making, at a time when there was, and would continue to be, enslaved people held in Vermont. In fact, Whitfield said that slavery in Vermont was actually eased out of existence over thirty years, between the 1770s and 1810.[103]

But the emancipation of Mattis and her daughter, Nancy, brings up plenty of questions. What became of them once they were free? Vermont's progressive constitution notwithstanding, enslaved people and maybe even formerly enslaved people arguably had more to gain from aligning with the British, especially if Great Britain won the war. As Judith Van Buskirk noted, in 1775, the Virginia royal governor John Murrary, the Earl of Dunmore, had issued a proclamation encouraging American enslaved people to bear arms and join His Majesty's Crown and dignity and "reap their own destiny." This was meant to encourage Black insurrections, and it led to a conscious effort to not enlist new Black volunteers in the Continental army.[104] In fact, Van Buskirk's research describes examples of enslaved people who ran away to find work with the British army. When the British army invaded New York City and White Americans left, many enslaved people were left behind to stay with their masters' homes. And in addition to more offers of safe harbors and opportunities for Black people with the British, Van Buskirk quotes Black abolitionists as saying that, as time went on, Great Britain did vastly more to abolish enslavement than America.

In November 1777, what would the options have been for Dinah Mattis? Before the Underground Railroad existed, were there employers who would pay former enslaved people fair wages and offer a new start? Did Lord Dunmore's appeal of more safety, security and opportunity lure Mattis toward New York? The choices for a free Black woman with a two-month-old daughter in Vermont, without a family, peer group, resources or employment opportunities in a difficult economy were limited. In 1777, Vermont was a brave little republic without a lot of resources or currency, and despite its new constitution, not everyone would have been respectful of the status of a former enslaved person. And since Mattis's daughter was under the age of eighteen, technically, she could have been legally enslaved again.

Attempting to track down the history of Dinah and Nancy Mattis is a frustrating endeavor. Harvey Amani Whitfield agreed. In his words, "It can be *very* difficult to trace enslaved Black people, or those who became free in early North America." Whitfield suggested that it is possible Mattis stayed with Allen, given that that was a common outcome with former enslaved people in New England.[105] Local Clarendon historian Bob Underhill concurred with Whitfield, adding, "Former slaves became almost invisible, and most of them had good reason to be living on the fringes. Given the general turmoil of the time, they could have gone almost anywhere without note being made of their presence, perhaps even to Canada."[106]

Dawn Hance, another historian who has researched and written several early Vermont town histories, offered another possibility. Hance says it was customary for towns to "bound out" people who didn't have money to those who were willing to take them in. In this scenario, towns would pay residents to take people in, usually to the lowest bidder. And it was common practice for towns to do this in the 1700s and 1800s. This practice continued when towns started building poorhouses in the nineteenth century. If Mattis was bound out, she might have worked on a farm or in some other capacity, and she possibly earned a small compensation along with room and board.[107] The research continues, but so far, the next chapters of Dinah and Nancy Mattis's lives remain an unsolved mystery. However, there is one disconcerting possibility found in a story that illustrates the elusiveness of abolition in Vermont. Seven years after Dinah Mattis was set free by Allen, a Black woman named Dinah was sold to a man in Vermont.

A woman named Dinah Mason White was enslaved by a man named White in Charlestown, New Hampshire, which was just over the bridge from Springfield, Vermont. She was purchased by Stephen Jacob in 1783, six years after Dinah Mattis was emancipated by Allen. Dinah served Jacob and his family for seventeen years in Windsor at his large State Street house until 1800. In fact, census records show that Jacob enslaved two people at that time. Jacob, who was a Dartmouth- and Yale-educated attorney and Supreme Court justice, purchased Dinah in direct violation of Vermont's Constitution.[108]

Dinah Mason White was eventually beset with health problems that included blindness, and Jacob kicked her out. The Town of Windsor sued Jacob for money to support Dinah. Jacob argued that she was free to come and go as she pleased. Jacob recused himself for the court case that was brought by the Town of Windsor regarding Dinah's care. Scholars have concluded that Dinah was a de facto enslaved person. The court held in Jacob's favor, although it affirmed that enslavement was unconstitutional in Vermont. The fallacious logic of the court held that, since slavery was illegal, Dinah couldn't have possibly been an enslaved person. Therefore, Jacob was found innocent.

Records show that Jacob paid some of Dinah's medical bills, and she received help from others in the community. But during the early 1800s, Dinah was "warned out," or kicked out of town several times. She died in 1809, a ward of the town, and was buried in a coffin in an unmarked grave.[109]

The research shows that Stephen Jacob's Dinah was born in 1753, and at the time of her purchase, she was named Dinah Mason White.[110] Enslaved people often took the surnames of their owners. Could it be this was the same Dinah whom Ebenezer had emancipated? That would solve one mystery. But if this is the case, we are still left with unanswered questions about Dinah Mattis's daughter, Nancy.

Let's hope that this was not how the story of Dinah and Nancy Mattis ended. Today, the standard of proof of their identity would be DNA evidence, but that would be impossible to find. Given the fact that Vermont had a population of only eighty-five thousand in 1800, the unpopularity of enslavement and knowing the obstacles Dinah would have faced, the Windsor story is a fairly plausible outcome of Dinah Mattis's manumission.

After Allen's performance at the Battle of Bennington, his capture of Mount Defiance, recon work at Fort Ticonderoga, rearguard capture and emancipation of the Mattises, he was commissioned as a major in Warner's Regiment and as a colonel in the state militia.

Although Fort Ticonderoga might have been useful as an enduring base, the Americans didn't have the money or military personnel to permanently occupy and defend the fort, Crown Point or other large military fortifications. Once the Pawlet expedition ended and the rangers' deployments expired, they returned to their farms and taverns with new tales of patriotism, commando operations and, this time, the liberation of enslaved people. But even though it was 1777 and Burgoyne had surrendered, the people of Vermont were still not safe. The Revolutionary War was far from over, and life in Vermont was still dangerous. Their survival was at stake.

8

TREACHERY AND SPIES

Another assignment in 1778 put Allen in charge of the small fort in New Haven, just above the Otter Creek Falls (later to become Vergennes, Vermont). It is important to keep in mind that Vermont had declared itself a separate republic by this time. New York was having a hard time accepting that new reality, since it believed it had legal ownership of Vermont. What events led up to Allen's mission at the fort in New Haven? The settlement of New Haven Falls was similar to a sometimes-violent ping pong game that lasted over ten years.

Back in 1769, a few families had moved north from Salisbury, Connecticut, and settled near the falls in New Haven. There, they cleared land and built dwellings and a sawmill. Not long afterward, Colonel Reid of New York arrived with a group of armed settlers and claimed the land on both sides of Otter Creek for a distance of two miles, based on New York grants.[111] Colonel Reed ejected the settlers, moved his own New York settlers into the area and built more houses and a gristmill. Before long, the Yorkers were, in turn, dispossessed by Ethan Allen and his Green Mountain Boys. Their houses and gristmill were destroyed, and the rightful owners were put back in possession of their property. Then, in July 1773, Colonel Reid arrived again with a number of Scottish immigrants, expelled the first settlers and repaired the mill.

When word of this reached Bennington, Ethan Allen and his Boys headed back to New Haven Falls and forcibly reinstated their friends. They broke the millstones and threw them over the falls. They also erected a blockhouse and garrisoned it with a small party under the command of none other than Ebenezer Allen. Allen ordered scout patrols around the falls area for as long as they were needed to deter further interference. Life was good until Allen left town for another urgent assignment. This time, by the late 1770s, Tory Justus Sherwood and a crew of followers broke up the settlement again and evicted the original settlers.

Who was Justus Sherwood? Sherwood was a Connecticut native, former Green Mountain Boy turned traitor and British Loyalist. Sherwood, who was about Allen's age, had been one of the founding members of the Green Mountain Boys; he was a brother-in-arms and a personal friend of Ethan, Ira, Ebenezer, Seth Warner and the whole gang. They had fought off the hated Yorkers and their repressive lawmen for years. Sherwood was a religious man who was well read and a thoughtful intellectual.

Sherwood had lived in Arlington and was part of the posse that had rescued Remember Baker after Yorkers had set his house on fire and assaulted him and his family. Baker, with his wife and kids, had to jump out of his burning house and into deep snow during that attack. His wife's arm was permanently injured in the fall, and Baker had a thumb cut off by a sword in the attack. The Yorkers arrested Baker, who was bleeding profusely, and carried him off in a wagon toward Albany, New York. Sherwood was part of the posse of Green Mountain Boys that rescued Baker just east of Albany on the trail and brought him back to Arlington.

In 1774, Justus Sherwood built a log cabin in New Haven, Vermont, just six miles southeast of Vergennes and a mile from Little Otter Creek in New Haven. There, he planted an apple orchard, where he lived with his wife, Sarah. As the first proprietor's clerk of New Haven, in 1774, the town council selected him as an "adventurer," presumably in the hopes that he would offer them some protection, along with the likes of fellow ruffians Ethan Allen and the other Green Mountain Boys. In return, the adventurers each received land grants of 150 acres on the condition that they improve the land within a year. But as time went on, Sherwood's beliefs led to him arguing with his neighbors about the Revolution. In his view, the longer the hostilities went on, the harder it was to accept an all-out revolution against the British. Over time, he became more and more conflicted. By 1776, when the Declaration of Independence was signed, Sherwood had decided that he was flatly against taking up arms against Great Britain. He rode to Crown Point and declared his allegiance to the king. Of course, this turn of events did not sit well with the Green Mountain Boys, and they were sure to let him know it.[112]

Shortly after his enlistment in the British army, a group of armed men showed up at Sherwood's door, and his cabin was ransacked, terrifying his pregnant wife and child. A few weeks later, another unit of the Green Mountain Boys, or the Arlington Mob, as some called them, showed up and moved right in with them, helping themselves to food and hanging out to intimidate his family. The bullying and intimidation did not sit right with Sherwood, but there was more to come. After being arrested by the Boys, tried and convicted as a Tory spy, he was whipped with sticks and sentenced to life in prison in the eighty-foot-deep Simsbury Mine, an abandoned copper mine in Connecticut. This fate would have led to an agonizing demise in Sherwood's fortunes.

Keep in mind that Ethan Allen had owned a mine in his younger days, before he came north to Bennington. These incidents had a particular Green Mountain Boy flavor to them. Allen had been ordered to do scouting assignments in New Haven at that time, and based on what Sherwood would later say in his letters to Governor Haldiman in Quebec, Ebenezer Allen played a role in Sherwood's humiliation.

When all seemed lost, Sherwood managed to escape captivity before his arrival at the mine. He quickly attracted about forty other Tory buddies and hid in the mountains he knew well for a few weeks. He eventually found his way to Crown Point, which, at the time, was stationed with a British garrison. In the meantime, his wife, Sarah Sherwood, and their two kids managed to escape to Bennington, near her family, and they eventually found their way to the safety of Crown Point. From there, Sherwood joined the British army and served as a scout. He then hitched a ride north to Canada with Sir Guy Carleton. Carleton had just defeated Benedict Arnold's fleet at the Battle of Valcour and chased Arnold's battered fleet southward and was taking a victory lap around the lake before heading to St. Johns, Quebec. The British were feeling pretty confident at that point, as they then controlled the lake with impunity.

It is fair to say that the Green Mountain Boys, including Ebenezer Allen, had a deep contempt for Sherwood, especially since he had once been one of them before renouncing their commitment against tyranny and becoming a bitter enemy. It was inconceivable to them how one of them could not only switch allegiances but also join the British secret service and work for the ruthless Governor General Haldimand, but that is exactly what he did.

Although Sherwood led raids of destruction, killing and kidnapping on Vermont settlers for years, he may have possessed a shred of humanity. In one example, he led a raiding party of Natives and Tories who were all painted to look like Natives on the town of Hubbardton on July 6 and 7, 1777. This raid occurred simultaneously with Seth Warner's rearguard retreat from Ticonderoga and Mount Independence to Hubbardton and the resulting Battle of Hubbardton. Sherwood's raiding party marched into Hubbardton and took four men prisoners: Benjamin and Uriah Hickcock, Henry Keeler and Elijah Kellogg. Benjamin Hickcock had a compact physique and managed to escape as they were all being led back through the thick woods. He returned to his home and, on the following night, left Hubbardton with his own family and his brother Uriah's family.

Sherwood spent the day lurking on Hubbardton Mountain during the Battle at Hubbardton. The next day, July 7, Sherwoood and his men captured Samuel Churchill and his family by surprise. They plundered the house of their provisions and clothing. Sherwood ordered the women and children to get out because he was going to burn the house down. After the women begged and pleaded with him, he relented and spared the home.

The Molly Stark House in Salisbury, Vermont, which was built and frequented by Green Mountain Boys. It is similar to other eighteenth-century cabins in Vermont. *Courtesy of Don Shall.*

During the raid, the father of the Churchill family, Samuel Churchill, was tied to a tree as his captors piled brush around his feet. The raiders taunted him in an attempt to pressure him to reveal his stores of flour, accusing him of holding out. They ignited the brush and continued to question him for three or four hours under the threat of burning him alive.

Finally, they killed his cattle and hogs and took as much meat as they could carry, along with the prisoners, back to Fort Ticonderoga. Sherwood then sent Churchill and Uriah Hickcock to work at Ticonderoga. They were stationed on a work detail below the fort, boating wood across Lake Champlain. Eventually, the British let their guard down and left one soldier to supervise the two men. Churchill and Hickock eventually persuaded their soldier guard to desert with them, and the two men returned to their home in search of their families. It took them three weeks to find their way back.[113]

ENFORCEMENT ACTIONS

Between 1778 and 1780, Allen had plenty of work to keep him busy. While he wasn't designing, building and commanding forts, he was ordered to conduct dozens of missions for the safety council. These missions included the aforementioned Tinmouth and New Haven assignments and protecting Patriot Vermonters in various ways. In one case, in 1779, Allen, Ethan and one hundred Green Mountain Boys arrested thirty men in Cumberland County (now in New Hampshire) who refused to recognize the authority of the new Republic of Vermont. They were all hauled to Westminster to stand trial.

This particular episode began with a Loyalist resident in Guilford, Vermont, near Brattleboro, who refused to be drafted into the militia. As a result, he was assessed the fine of one cow. When the sheriff arrived to confiscate the cow, the man was surrounded by a large group of Loyalist buddies, and the sheriff was subsequently scared off. Ethan Allen was alerted of the scofflaws and commanded to apprehend them by future governor Thomas Chittenden. The Green Mountain Boys wasted no time in getting to work.[114]

When the Boys appeared and began hauling away the scofflaws to trial, the frightened victims sent New York governor Clinton an urgent message asking for help, "Otherwise our persons and property must be at the disposal of Ethan Allin [*sic*], which is more to be dreaded than death with all its terrors."[115] By then, Clinton was well acquainted with the Green Mountain Boys, and he wanted nothing to do with the situation.

These infractions occurred over and over again and became known as the "Great Cow War." Allen's enforcers kept pretty busy. When the Loyalists went to trial, the judge in Westminster admonished them and levied small fines against them. Governor Chittenden subsequently pardoned them, believing that he needed to demonstrate his power and sovereignty of the state while also not overreacting to his citizens.

Even though the Green Mountain Boys were doing a great job of harassing Loyalists and keeping Yorkers in check, Vermonters were not feeling adequately protected from the devastating raids in their settlements. An April 26, 1778 letter to George Washington from American general Philip Schuyler gives us an idea of the kind of routine missions that Captain Allen was running. In that letter, Schuyler said:

> *Five or seven of the enemy's largest vessels on Champlain are arrived at Tyonderoga and, it is said, have debarked a body of troops at that place, another body of about five hundred landed opposite Crown Point, and in their march towards Mount Independence, fell in with Captain Allen, who commanded a scouting party of one hundred militia. The latter have been obliged to retreat with some loss.*
>
> *I do not apprehend that any considerable body of the enemy will attempt to penetrate into the country, at least not until they are reinforced from Europe, but scalping parties will probably commit depredations, and such is the dread of the inhabitants on that account that they are already leaving their plantations, not a single soldier being left for their protection.*[116]

Unfortunately, Schuyler underestimated the destruction Carleton's raid would leave. In early November, Major Christopher Carleton's party of two hundred troops, including Loyalists and Natives, under orders from the British commander General Haldimand in Quebec, went ashore from Otter Creek in Middlebury, and they proceeded to "scorch and burn" everything near Otter Creek, all the way to the lake. This included the New Haven Blockhouse. They took dozens of prisoners to Quebec as well. Petersen documented that, of the over thirty prisoners taken, a few escaped, some died in captivity and others returned to live traumatized lives after two or three years in captivity. The raids catalyzed the fort building frenzy that ensued from 1778 to 1780.

Two years later, in 1780, Allen's scouting party discovered another invasion by Major Carleton. The force included eight large vessels, a number of bateaus and Natives in canoes, with a total of around one thousand men near Chimney Point, and it was headed for Fort Ticonderoga. Allen sent a message of the invasion to Ethan, who called out all of the state militia. Carleton's forces subsequently stood down and passed down the lake without further attacks. But as we shall see, the Allens had a directive for a ceasefire from the secret cabinet. It is possible that Carleton was turned away by the ceasefire and not so much by the threat of combat with Herrick's Rangers.[117]

SPIES, SECRET NEGOTIATIONS AND KIDNAPPINGS

By 1780, Captain Sherwood was a British secret agent living in Canada. Sherwood would soon be the Quebec governor's main northeast negotiator, operating out of the Lake Champlain Islands (North Hero). The British wanted to entice Vermont to become a colony of Great Britain. Benedict Arnold, who became another high-profile traitor in 1780; British general Haldimand, who was the governor of Canada; and Sherwood all agreed that Vermont was ripe for joining the British side and giving up its military operations. According to Elliot Cohen and other historians, the British surmised they could pay the Continental army's salaries, which were a couple of years in arrears, and win Vermonters over to become a territory of His British Excellence, King George III. Ethan, Ira and Joseph Fay were all actively negotiating with Sherwood over the next few years.

But the British strategy also had another phase. The British secret service embarked on a kidnapping program in which they would kidnap high-profile Vermonters. Sherwood was sending out parties of agents to gather intelligence in the northern colonies and to kidnap prominent Whigs.[118] Raids by British troops and Natives were still in force as well, particularly in the northern parts of the republic. And Sherwood was in a unique position to manage prisoner exchanges in the Vermont Republic.

Across the lake in Point au Fer, New York (just north of Plattsburgh), a British blockhouse was built in 1780. Roger Stevens, another Patriot-turned-traitor Tory was sent with his new recruits to Point au Fer to establish an observation outpost. This was to be the most advanced outpost of the British network to obtain intelligence and more Loyalist recruits from Vermont and New York. Stevens was there for four months during the winter of 1780, and although he worked for Sherwood as a spy, Sherwood had a low opinion of him. Sherwood felt Roger Steven's effectiveness as a spy was vitiated by his "dancing and frolicking with girls." Stevens

Governor General Haldimand of Quebec. *Public domain.*

drowned four years after the war ended while he was duck hunting in Canada. In the meantime, Sherwood was planning to build a similar blockhouse due east on the Vermont side of the lake.

Under Haldimand's orders, in 1781, Sherwood built the Loyal Block House on Dutchman's Point (later to be named Blockhouse Point) in what is now North Hero. Keep in mind that the land in Vermont was still locked in a war and power struggle with Britain hanging around, especially on the lake. The controversial negotiations proceeded between the British general Haldimand and Ethan, Ira and Vermont secretary of state Joseph Fay, who was the son of Jonas Fay. And the nexus for those negotiations was in the Champlain Islands, located just a few miles north of Allen's new homestead in Two Heroes (today's South Hero). Allen had butted heads with Sherwood in New Haven, North Hoosick and other locales. According to North Hero historian Mary Jane Healy, two years later, in 1783, the Vermont assembly voted to give more than three hundred property lots to the Green Mountain Boys in sixty-four-acre parcels. The land records show that in the same year the Treaty of Paris was signed, the blockhouse lot was sold to Justus Sherwood by Joseph Fay.[119]

The Loyal Block House was built and sat elevated on a bluff on the southern point of North Hero Island, overlooking the lake highway, during the summer of 1781. The building was a typical two-story blockhouse design. Its original size has not been determined. Many blockhouses during the Revolution had a sixteen-by-twenty-foot footprint, were two stories high and had up to thirty-two portholes. They served as arsenals and meeting places and protected fortifications from attacks. The North Hero Blockhouse must have been larger, as it housed a garrison of up to fifty men, according to Ian Pemberton.[120]

Today, a Sons of the American Revolution historical marker and flags, which were installed in 1914, remain at the North Hero Blockhouse site, which is now owned privately. A garrison at the site would have needed outbuildings and watercraft, and we know that it was used by the British for at least fifteen years. North Hero town records note that the relations

A 1955 aerial photograph of the North Hero Blockhouse, the headquarters of Secret Agent Justus Sherwood and a British garrison, taken by Mike Costello. *Courtesy of Mary Jane Healy.*

between the British soldiers and settlers were always cordial and respectful, even though not everyone was impressed with Captain Sherwood.

In a karmic twist, Allen was ordered to provide protective security for Sherwood during the negotiations. After all, Sherwood was still despised as a traitor for his wicked deeds during the raids on Vermont towns. He needed diplomatic immunity in order to survive. If anyone could have ensured his safety, Allen was the man for the job. But according to Sherwood's journal, there was no love lost between the two men. In a letter to Governor Haldimand, Sherwood wrote that Ebenezer Allen had mistreated him in the past, and it was so painful to see him that he could hardly treat him with common civility.[121] Apparently, Allen enjoyed aggravating Sherwood.[122] Author Mary Beacock Fryer recently wrote a historical fiction account about Sherwood called *The Buckskin Pimpernel*. In real life, Sherwood drowned in 1795 after falling of a logging raft in the St. Lawrence River.

ALLEN'S ROLE IN THE SECRET NEGOTIATIONS

To summarize the state of affairs in Vermont in a very compact nutshell: the Declaration of Independence had been signed and approved, and Great Britain was not impressed. Hostilities with the British and Native populations continued for years, even long after the Treaty of Paris was signed in 1783, supposedly ending the war. Vermont had recently applied to Congress for the recognition of its statehood and was denied. Warner's Continental troops hadn't seen a paycheck for a while, and British governor General Haldimand and others believed that the Vermonters were ripe for the financial rewards and security benefits of joining Britain. Ethan, Ira and others actively promoted this possibility. Historians debate whether the Allens were using the British negotiations as leverage to scare Congress into awarding Vermont statehood, or if the Allens actually saw joining Great Britain as a viable option to further their own commercial enterprises. It is possible that their interests were fueled by a bit of both.[123]

George Washington had spoken of a "mercenary spirit" that pervaded the war and the possibility that it might lead to disaster.[124] Perhaps the Haldimand negotiations belied a mercenary spirit that was alive in Ira and Ethan Allen. Did they push the New Hampshire land grants and fight off the New York grants out of their own mercenary interests? Did they negotiate with the British in the hopes of better gaining fortunes from British sterling and gold in the midst of their sagging homegrown economies in frontier Vermont?

Regardless of the hindsight and present-day ethical optics, the logistical issues of secretly negotiating with the British were complicated. Would Ethan and Ira be tried or even hanged for treason? Letters show that some Vermonters were openly accusing them of treason. What about the continued British hostilities, attacks, raids and kidnappings—wouldn't they hamper negotiations at the very least? Would Sherwood become a target for violence by the Vermont Patriots he had deserted? We can see why Sherwood would have needed protection in the 1780s, amid the continued conflict in Vermont.

Ironically, Sherwood proposed kidnapping Ebenezer Allen, Governor Thomas Chittenden and Jacob Bayley, a former British-turned-American officer who founded Newbury, Vermont. Sherwood's reasoning was, if these prominent men were taken, it would be easier to get Vermonters to agree to British rule. A mission to kidnap Bayley failed when Bayley was forewarned and escaped, although the attempt resulted in other men being shot and killed in collateral fire. An operation to kidnap American general

Philip Schuyler in Albany, New York, failed as well because he had posted six guards who resisted the would-be abductors. We don't know if there was an active plot to kidnap Ebenezer. We can surmise that if Sherwood had made an attempt, the kidnappers would have gotten more than they bargained for, and there would be a story to tell.

For several years, Sherwood ran an elaborate organization of informants, spies and counterspies that ranged from New York City to Quebec. During the early 1780s, the Loyal Blockhouse had a steady stream of visitors, and for a while, it was a garrison, the negotiations meeting site and a station for spies who were coming and going. Sherwood wrote questionnaires for his spies. One spy, John Savage, was given a list that included:

- *Where is Washington's army stationed, and in what numbers?*
- *Where are the French troops and in what number?*
- *What is the present disposition of the populace to the French?*
- *What is the present disposition of the populace to a reunion with Great Britain?*
- *What is the disposition of the other states towards Vermont?*
- *In what manner are the rebel troops clothed, provisioned, and paid?*[125]

Apparently, Savage found evidence of considerable problems with morale, both in the civilian and military populations.

In the meantime, General Washington was clearly out of the loop with the Haldimand negotiations, as we will find out later. A so-called alarming letter from Captain Ebenezer Allen to Captain Jesse Safford at Bethel was passed up to Washington; it referred to a ceasefire in Vermont that was going to be used to facilitate negotiations with the British. General Ethan Allen had asked Ebenezer Allen, who was stationed at Fort Vengeance in Pittsford, to ensure a temporary ceasefire on the other side of the mountain, id est, eastern Vermont. Joseph Marsh, who sent the letter to Washington, warned that the Vermont negotiations might be worse than the incident of "treachery" at West Point. What was the treachery?

In September 1780, Benedict Arnold scheduled a breakfast date with General Washington. Washington didn't know that the breakfast date was really ground zero of a secret British plot to kidnap him and simultaneously capture the fortification at West Point. Had Arnold pulled this off, it could have been a game-changing coup d'état for the British. After all, West Point was one of America's most strategic positions, as it guarded the Hudson River. The Hudson River was not only the main transportation corridor, but it was also essential for communication and military operations between the southern and northern colonies. The only reason the plot failed was that the British ship *Vulture*, which carried the attacking force, failed to receive its final orders to transport the invaders. The plot was only exposed after a communication was intercepted explaining the operation. By that time, Benedict Arnold had escaped, but one of his coconspirators was caught and hanged.[126]

The following is a letter that was sent to General Washington with an extract of the correspondence from Captain Ebenezer Allen to Safford:

To George Washington from Joseph Marsh, 3 November 1780
Dresden on the New Hampshire Grants Novr 3d A.D. 1780

Sir,

May it please your Excellency—we have, this moment, received a paper attested by Capt. Safford of which the enclosed is a copy—its contents are to us unintelligible and alarming—we know not what construction to put on it, unless a negociation [sic] is on foot for a separate peace for the new state, which we have heard has been threatened if Congress should not acknowledge the independence of Vermont and admit them to union—under these apprehensions we send the enclosed to your Excellency, as the consequences of such negotiation may be speedily fatal to the settlements contiguous to Connecticut River and more dangerous to the United States than the late treachery at West-Point.

The enemy in number three hundred destroyed Royalton and part of Sharon in this vicinity about a fortn't ago and took thirty prisoners—scouts lately returned from Onion River discovered last week about one thousand of the enemy near its confluence whose object is supposed to be [Cohos] or this place—our situation, at best, is critical, and we are in danger of being totally destroyed soon unless assistance is granted for our defence [sic].

Our apprehensions respecting the enclosed may be groundless, but our fears are great. I write this on behalf of the general committee on the grants contiguous to Connecticut River, and have the honor to be with highest sentiments of duty and esteem, sir, your excellency's most obedient and most humble servant,

Joseph Marsh Chairman
DLC: Papers of George Washington.

Enclosure
Extract of a letter from Major Allen, dated Fort Vengeance Octr 30th A.D.
1780—to Capt. Jesse Safford at Bethel-Fort

30 October 1780

Dear Capt.
I received a letter from General Allen last evening informing that the evening
before he received a flag from the British troops at Crown Point with letters
of importance from the commander in chief at Quebec—Major Carlton
hath pledged his faith that all hostilities on his part shall cease during the
negociation [sic], *and he expects the same on our part—you are therefore*
carefully to observe the rules of war and give strict orders to your scouts and
troops to govern themselves accordingly.

A copy of this letter you will forward to the troops stationed on your side
of the mountain in this state—I shall inform you of every move necessary
for you moving on this side of the mountain.

If the spirit of this letter were made known to the inhabitants on your
side of the mountain it would be well. I am, dear sir, your humble servant,

Ebenezer Allen Major Comdt

The above is a true copy from an extract attested by the above name Jesse
Safford commanding a party of men raised by the new state and stationed
at Bethel on White River.
Taken by desire of the general committee on the New Hampn. Grants
contiguous to Connecticut River—Attestn.
Bezr: Woodward Clerk [127]

As we can see from Joseph Marsh's letter, Washington was aware of the
"grave threat if Congress should not acknowledge the independence of
Vermont and admit them to union." The southern states resisted Vermont's
statehood. General Washington had plenty on his plate at the time, but one
has to wonder if Washington was doing any political arm-twisting with
Congress to get Vermont admitted to the Union. Eleven years passed before
statehood was finally granted to Vermont.

Economic Hardships Erode Patriotism

As if the perils of the cold, hungry northern frontier were not enough, the postwar economy further squeezed settlers in Vermont. The realities of survival in the wilderness on largely unceded Native land and in the postwar economic recession created crises and a conflict of commitment for many Vermonters. In fact, evidence shows that many Vermonters depended on British trade from across the border in Canada for survival. Jason Barney's book *The War of 1812 in Northern Vermont* documents just how dependent northern Vermonters were on Canadian trade. As a result, trading with Canada, whether it was legal or not, was a way of survival for many in northern Vermont. In the dismal postwar economy, Vermonters needed buyers for their beef cattle and timber in order to eat. And cash was a rare commodity, so a lot of business transactions were conducted with barterable goods and promissory notes.

When Allen sold his estate in Tinmouth, he took beef in payment; then he attempted to sell it privately to a buyer in Canada via a shipment from Crown Point. Since the British were still hanging around the lake, impressing Americans and controlling transportation, any trade that would benefit the British would probably not help the Patriot cause of freedom. Trade that benefitted Canada also helped the British cause, as they needed Vermont's building materials and food. Even though trade with Canada was a means of survival, it was a "no-no," and Colonel Allen found himself in hot water. Also, historian John Duffy mentioned that Allen seemed to be involved in a counterfeiting scheme with a cattle-trading colleague, Azariah Pritchard. At the time, Governor Chittenden had referred to American beef as contraband. Meanwhile, Ethan and Ira were negotiating with General Haldimand for free trade for cattle and timber with Canada. Finally, in 1784, Haldimand relented and relaxed the prohibition on shipping Vermont cattle into Canada. But free trade was not all Ethan and Ira were negotiating for.

As historian John Duffy noted, the secret cabinet of Ethan, Ira Allen, Joseph Fay and others actually promoted the practice of settling Loyalists in northern Vermont and, especially, in the border town of Alburgh so they would have a population that would be more amenable to free trade and other British-friendly policies.[128] Ethan must have trusted the British negotiator and spy James Savage, since Savage reported the following conjecture to Sherwood:

It is determined in the private cabinet of Vt. to give every possible encouragement to loyal subjects in the Colonies to remove into the northern parts of Vt. and on this island [North Hero], by this policy (A) [Allen] thinks there may soon be a party found in opposition to Congress, sufficient to bring about revolution in favor of Vt.'s uniting with Canada and becoming a British Gov't. [129]

As we know, the Haldimand negotiations failed to produce an alliance between Vermont and Great Britain, and Vermont was finally admitted to the Union in 1791. Ebenezer Allen's multifaceted talents were in great demand in the Champlain Islands. By the mid-1780s, he was a founding father of the booming community of South Hero, an employer and an integral part of building a community in "Two Heroes." He immediately started working on construction projects and side hustles that would turn out to be very fruitful.

TURBULENT TIMES

B y the end of the 1770s, Colonel Allen had been heavily engaged in Vermont Council on Safety assignments, and in 1779, he was concurrently deeded land in Fair Haven and in the Champlain Islands, along with 359 other Revolutionary War veterans, by Governor Thomas Chittenden. The charter for the islands was filed under the name of "Two Heroes," ostensibly for Ethan and Ira Allen. Ebenezer Allen moved northward to be one of the first White settlers on the island, probably arriving as early as 1779 and building a log house in the dense forest near a south-facing bluff on the lake.

Those who are familiar with South Hero know that there are a number of factors that evoke a magnificent ambiance on Allen's Point, where he settled. The place boasts breathtaking views of the Green Mountains of Vermont and the high peaks of the Adirondack Mountains of northern New York State. A banana belt microclimate in the area offers a longer growing season than the rest of the north country latitudes. The freshwater access, enchanting light, abundant wildlife and fertile soils of South Hero all conspire to create an alluring place to prosper.

Allen's grandson would write that Allen had traveled up from Tinmouth on snowshoes along the Vermont side of the lake to St. Albans, Vermont. Then he crossed over to the center of the islands on ice. There, he, Alexander Gordon and Enos Wood drew lots to determine who should have the first, second and third choice of location, as the islands had not been surveyed yet. Wood drew the first choice and Gordon drew the second choice, and they

The 1783 log cabin of Jedediah Hyde, a neighbor of Ebenezer Allen. *Courtesy of the Library of Congress.*

selected lots on the north island and on the north end of the south island, respectively. Allen chose the southern tip of the south island of Two Heroes as the site of his homestead. This pristine setting in northern Vermont would become his stomping ground for work and family life for the next two decades. Although Allen's whereabouts at any given time were scattered and hard to pin down, especially from 1779 to 1781, there is strong evidence that he had built a log cabin on the island by 1779.[130]

Although there has been some controversy surrounding exactly when Colonel Allen arrived on the island and built the log house, the preponderance of the evidence points to the year 1779. Based on accounts that are summarized in *The History of Grand Isle*, these arguments support his arrival in 1779.

> • *Nearly all of the oldest citizens of the island, now called Grand Isle, during the 1800s agreed that Colonel Allen, Lamberton Allen and Alexander Gordon were the very first White settlers and only inhabitants of the south island, with Lamberton arriving a few months later than Colonel Allen and Gordon.*

- *According to Professor George Allen, his father, Lamberton Allen, one of the original settlers who arrived on the island in 1780, had stayed at Colonel Allen's home after his arrival. The following winter, he lived in a house that Allen had built for someone else.*
- *Professor Allen also explained that it was remembered that Lamberton had arrived in South Hero just before the famous "dark day," May 19, 1780. This was corroborated by another resident who remembered hearing the family of Ebenezer's colleague Alexander Gordon relate that the two men had resided on the island before the dark day occurred.[131]*

The dark day in 1780 was a defining moment in history—a well-documented account of complete darkness settling over all of New England for a day. Of course, at a time when people had no means of getting timely emergency information, let alone coherent scientific atmospheric observations, it was terrifying. Many people feared it was the end of the world, and they prepared for the worst.

For example, it is documented that people came out into the city streets that day and prepared for the moment of the apocalypse. The event prompted some people to join the Shakers, an obscure splinter group

The interior of the Hyde cabin. The Hydes were contemporaries of Ebenezer Allen, and they lived on the same island. *Courtesy of Lucille Campbell and the Grand Isle Historical Society.*

of Quakers who preached celibacy and, as a result, have since become extinct. The dark day is believed to have been caused by massive regional land-clearing and the burning of forest fires in the Northeast and Canada combined with a fog.[132]

The dark day serves as a timestamp for when Allen, according to several accounts, built his log home on Allen's Point and, at least on a part-time basis, inhabited the island with a few other hardy souls. This would fit the pattern of his prior residences in Poultney and Tinmouth, which were not constantly occupied by him. To put it mildly, he was very active between 1779 and 1781. Although, by 1780, a lot of his activities appeared to migrate to the Champlain Valley.

WITHOUT CIVIL AND MILITARY LAW

Allen's name and reputation had preceded him, and his prosperity grew. There are no further records of his active continental military duties after 1781. Allen was very successful as an entrepreneur. Despite the lure of British money, there is no evidence that he felt any Loyalist yearnings. And some residents of the Champlain Islands area, particularly in the northern border area of Alburgh, were continually harassed by the British, who commanded the lake and Canadian border. The early justices of the peace and Deputy Sheriff Enos Wood were, on occasion, arrested and detained by British officers under charges of officiating for Vermont. Although they were threatened with imprisonment in Quebec, they were generally released without harm. It is interesting that, despite the harassment in Alburgh, there was not any mention of British bullying a few miles south in Allen's community of South Hero. However, that is not to say there wasn't a culture of lawlessness in the community.

One story, in particular, offers an example of life on the northern Vermont frontier before the wrinkles were ironed out of Vermont's legal and justice system. This anecdote comes by way of *The History of Grand Isle and Franklin Counties*, written by Reverend David Marvin of Alburgh. In 1792, Alburgh included Missisco Tongue (Alburgh Tongue) and Missisco Leg (Windmill Point), which were two prominent points of land on the lake in Alburgh; and as we shall see, they were the focus of some dramatic events. The anecdote involves a man who was known by the name of John Griggs; according to the Alburgh town records, he owned property in Alburgh up until 1798, when he met his tragic demise. But this particular incident occurred in 1781 on Windmill Point, which was a duty post near the Canadian border at the north end of Alburgh.

The story began with a man named Cheeseman, who had settled on a lot north of and next to the windmill, which was originally built by the French and renovated by settler Ephraim Mott. Cheeseman had cleared a few wooded acres, built a house and then returned to live in St. Johns, Quebec, which was about thirty miles due north of Alburgh. Cheeseman left a cow with his brother-in-law John Griggs. Griggs was supposed to settle a debt with the cow that was due to someone a few miles south in Grand Isle.

Here is where the story became a bit fuzzy. According to Reverend Marvin, Griggs settled on what had been known as the Samuel Mott place. It is not clear if Griggs had permission to settle there, if he was squatting on Mott's land, if there was some difference of opinion of ownership or if it was some other conflict altogether. Apparently, a posse of armed men, who were said to have been sent by Colonel Allen, showed up at Griggs's residence at sundown. It was a calm evening, and Griggs happened to be out in a boat with his fishing buddy Joshua Manning. Manning had been boarding with Griggs and clearing land on which he later settled.

As Manning and Griggs approached the shoreline in their boat, they could see the armed posse pulling up, mounted on their horses, and they overheard one of them talking about firing on them. Manning cried out, "For God's sake, gentlemen, don't fire. We're coming to shore as fast as we can." Then they heard, "I'll shoot the man in the bow." Another one said, "Fire!" A shotgun blast of buckshot hit Manning under the knee, severing his "cords" (probably his patellar tendon). Apparently, Manning never regained use of his leg after that and was "crippled for life," Marvin noted. "They failed to arrest Griggs—probably were too drunk." Marvin summarized the incident by saying, "It will be remembered that this was during the period when they were without law, civil or military."[133]

This account does not indict Allen, but it does at least show that people thought his involvement was within the realm of possibility. Alburgh was a Loyalist area, and the war was far from over in Vermont. We don't know if Allen was directly or indirectly involved in this incident; what protocols were followed by the posse, if any; whether the posse had specific orders or instructions; whether alcohol played a role; or if it would have mattered. Many years later, Griggs would become a fugitive and the victim at the center of a tragic murder investigation into the actions of the sheriff.

Struggling Settlers

Allen's new home was on Two Heroes, a double island situated twenty-six miles south of Alburgh. Even though the islands were an unspoiled wilderness not unlike the rest of Vermont, the winter was a harsh climate. And because of that, it was not necessarily the land of plenty—at least, not in the winter. Several accounts describe the initial island ecosystem as dense forests of hardwoods that were infested with wild animals. The earliest settlers constantly suffered from a lack of provisions, especially meat. Hunting and fishing provided the bulk of their food, and not all of the settlers were adept at procuring food, to say nothing about wilderness survival. The first dwellings on the islands were near water, and as Jedediah Hyde mentioned, the fastest communication of the day was by dugout canoe. Bilious and intermittent fevers (bacterial infections) were common and often proved fatal.

Jedediah Hyde's journal entry from Saturday, September 27, 1783, included the following:

> At about 10 o'clock, Col. ALLEN with Mr. BENNETT returned, the former being very unwell, and the whole very much beat out with their march across the woods. By Mr. BENNETT, I received a letter from Capt. HYDE, in which I can find no confirmation of Mr. SMITH's report concerning his coming on soon with provisions, but believe that he expects we can subsist on the wind....Mr. BENNETT informs me that he took aboard a small quantity of garden sauce for me, but having such an unlucky passage, had occasion to use all but about one mess (for which he has the thanks of his humble servant, the same as though they had all come safe to hand, and he is as welcome as a prince to those he made use of).[134]

Those who were fortunate to have wheat needed to travel to Whitehall or Granville, New York, across the lake to have it ground into flour. They could also have it ground by hand a little at a time. Thompson reported accounts of families during the years 1784–85 bordering on starvation, eating only two meals a day. In some cases, their diets came down to bread and milk.

Needing shoes and clothing, some settlers on the island gathered the funds they were able and placed them in the keeping of one of their trusty neighbors. The unnamed man rode on horseback to Bennington as the weather became colder to purchase a supply of shoes and much-needed clothing in order to outfit them in the extreme rigors of winter with windswept arctic-like conditions on the island. But for whatever reason, the neighbor did not return from his mission until weeks later, in the middle of December. By that time, many of the inhabitants had suffered severe frostbite.[135]

But each year, a few dozen more settlers arrived on the island, and the influx of new talent created more cooperative support and an economy of scale. In 1783, Allen brought lumber from a sawmill over the lake and to the island on a raft to build a frame house and expand his property. He unloaded the lumber, disassembled the raft and used it to build the frame house and barn. His acreage was soon to be known as Allen's Point in South Hero. He planted the island's first apple orchard; grew wheat, corn and other crops; and his farm thrived. He also built a blacksmith shop, and within a few years, hundreds of new settlers followed to populate the community that would become the town of South Hero. Allen is also credited with initiating the first apple production on Isle La Motte in 1790, and he was instrumental in setting up the orchards on that northernmost island.[136]

As was common practice, the town provided property for a clergyman in the early 1780s, and there were church services on the island after that. The First Congregational Church was formed in 1802, and the Methodist church, now known as the Old White Meeting House, was built in 1816 in South Hero, ten years after Allen's death. Although there were Calvinistic Methodists, it is not known whether the Methodist Church or prior ministers in the town espoused Calvinist beliefs. In 1787, Allen enlarged his own house again, constructed outbuildings and opened a public house.

The public house, commonly shortened to "pub," was sometimes called a tavern. In the eighteenth century, taverns were often inns or hotels where travelers could stay. We know that Allen owned a tavern next to his home, which offered lodging and dry goods, as well as food and drink.

ALLEN THE BUSINESSMAN

Allen also operated a ferry to the mainland during the warmer months; it ran from a landing near the present-day entrance to Skyland to Colchester Point, according to Allen's Point native Ron Phelps. The technology utilized by early ferries varied. Allen operated a flat-bottomed scow ferry to carry people, animals, wagons and carriages over the "reef" to Colchester, close to the current route of the quarry stone–filled Colchester Causeway railway bike path. Some of the two-mile crossing was fordable with reefs and sandbars, but a lot of it would have been perilous over deep water. Those who are familiar with Lake Champlain know that placid weather and gentle waves can turn deadly furious very quickly and unexpectedly. Choppy water with rolling waves in excess of four to six feet and greater are not uncommon, so the ferry business was no place for landlubbers.

In those days, ferrymen used poles, oars and sails to move boats across the water. And water offered the fastest transportation before and even after some roads had been cleared. Many personal accounts tell of ferries using oars in the 1700s to move animals to and from several different points in the islands.

Primitive roads were being cleared by the end of the century. Allen built the first road in South Hero, which ran from his place on Allen Point to Lamberton Allen's place on the west shore, now the Lake Champlain Transportation Ferry Docks. This road, which was wide enough to permit the width of two yoked oxen, would have followed what is now the current bike path and West Shore Road.

The typical tavern in the 1700s was a meeting place for town meetings, business deals, political discussions and military meetings. They typically offered store goods, food, wine, brandy, rum, beer and other beverages. It is widely established that alcohol was commonly used not only as a medicine, but also as a safer alternative to water and a regular dietary

A sketch of the South Hero Ebenezer Allen house at an unknown date. Speculation is that the inn and outbuildings were adjacent to the house. *Courtesy of the South Hero Historical Society.*

supplement. People drank while on the job, working in the fields and on military duty. There were no age limits for alcohol use, so young, old and even the clergy imbibed. Ales, apple and grape cider wine were common locally crafted drinks, all of which were made in Vermont and the rest of New England. Rum was distilled from molasses, which came from sugar cane that was grown in southern climates. Three of the common beverages referred to in the Green Mountain Boys' accounts included stonewalls, flips and punch.

THE HOSPITALITY BUSINESS

Although recipes varied from tavern to tavern, with local availability of ingredients and customs, one of the more popular refreshments was the stonewall. Stonewalls were made by combining dark rum and hard cider. Readers who have experienced the effects of combining two alcoholic potions together can appreciate the impact a few of those colonial cocktails would have had on the mind and body. This was a culture with little if any concern of the potential social, transportation or medical effects that we recognize today.

Another drink, called the flip, was a bit more complicated and might have relied on an acquired taste. The flip involved combining beaten eggs, rum and sugar or molasses with steaming heated beer. Then the mixture was poured back and forth between pitchers. Finally, a hot fire poker was inserted into the concoction to produce a frothy topping. It was a drink that was perfect for a winter evening in the north country. Flips have been compared to drinking liquified earth.[137]

Punch was usually made from wine, that is, fermented fruits. Often, the fortified wines, such as Port or Madeira, were used in punch, with lemon juice, sugar and nutmeg. Punch was made by the glass, not in a bowl.

We can also presume that since Allen grew his own crops, his bar menu included apple wine and spirits, as well as rum, ale and other choices that were seasonally plentiful at the time. We also know from the Allen papers that Claret, a French (red Bordeaux) wine, was very popular at the time. Allen's public house at his residence became a popular meeting and lodging place for travelers, and according to Barnes, he employed local people to work in his businesses.

Like most establishments, taverns attracted all kinds of characters, including the good, the bad and the evil. Alcohol, being a social lubricant, sometimes eroded men's inhibitions and led to heated discussions and confrontations. Allen's military bearing and reputation for order was well respected, and it is likely that brawling or other inappropriate behaviors were not tolerated in the least at the Two Heroes Tavern.

Colonel Allen quickly became a pillar of community service and served as the South Hero "proprietor's clerk," which was similar to the town clerk position, before the town was chartered in 1784. He was also selected as one of the town's two justices of the peace. One of the other justices who served South Hero was a man by the name of Colonel Stephen Pearl. Allen would later become embroiled as a defendant in a civil lawsuit against the plaintiff, Colonel Pearl. We will unravel more of that puzzling episode later.

Law and Order

In April 1784, Allen was appointed as a major in the Vermont militia, west of the Green Mountains. Among other duties, the governor and council resolved that Allen should take possession of the British Loyal Blockhouse that had been built by Justus Sherwood in North Hero as soon as it was evacuated by British troops. Perhaps the governor hoped that Allen could offer some persuasion, so to speak, to Sherwood and his minions to lose interest in the continued occupation of the garrison. Even though Vermont was admitted to the Union as the fourteenth state in 1791, the British didn't officially leave until 1796. Unlike the Loyal Blockhouse, other properties in the islands were changing hands very quickly.

Thomas Chittenden, a statesman, leader and Vermont governor from 1778 to 1789. *Public domain.*

Allen had other duties as well. Before the war, a man named Simon Metcalfe obtained a New York title for land in the Swanton area and had developed a farm on the Missisquoi River, where he employed three hundred Canadians in timber cutting. Metcalfe had been ejected by Ira Allen, who had procured a New Hampshire deed for the same land during the war. After the war, Metcalfe returned to resume business.

On July 5, 1784, Ebenezer wrote Simon Metcalfe:

Sir,
It is very unhappy that I have to send you this admontisement [sic] *but as I am orrther'd* [sic] *by the commander in cheef* [sic] *of this state to keep of all invaders north of Castleton east of the Greene Mountains and knowing the disposition of Newyork* [sic] *to wards of the free situations of this state brings me to warn you to quit the soil you protend* [sic] *to hold under Newyork* [sic] *forth with or I shall pay you as viset wich* [sic] *will be to put the old laws of the state in execution.*

Sind Ebr. Allen Colo.
Commanding from Castleton to Latude 45
East of the Green Mountains

Ebenezer made good on his warning. Ira Allen, assisted by brother Levi, prosecuted Metcalfe in a court in Arlington and had him evicted from his land in Swanton. Levi Allen, by the way, bought the entire town in 1773 then lost it in a tax sale in 1784 to his brother Ira.[138]

According to North Hero historian Mary Jane Healy, by the time the Champlain Islands' grants were made, many of the Champlain Islands grantees had already settled elsewhere. Consequently, they sold their island lots. But the Vermont assembly had levied a capital gains tax of one-half cent per acre in order to support a general fund for a prison and other projects. Many of the grantees had sold their lots without properly recording the sale or paying the tax. This would become a pervasive issue with all kinds of negative consequences. As a result of not being recorded or taxed, these lots were foreclosed.

Public auctions known as sheriff sales or vendues, in which the lots were auctioned off to the highest bidder, led to disputes over lots that appeared to have absentee or multiple owners. In 1785, at a vendue in Poultney, Allen bid on delinquent tax properties in South Hero that totaled 1,200 acres, and he bought eighteen of those deeds, which he later sold to others. These properties had been deeded to war veterans, and in many cases, the properties had never been settled. In the case of South Hero, deeded land needed to be occupied within a particular time period or the deeds would expire. Other well-known islanders, such as Jedediah Hyde and tax collector Alexander Gordon, were also in attendance at the auction in Poultney.

In October 1786, there were widespread economic difficulties among settlers, a scarcity of money and increasing taxation. That was the year of Shays's Rebellion in Massachusetts, and Vermont was experiencing its own protests, which were fueled by pervasive drunkenness, taxes, lawsuits and a bad economy, according to historians. There were insurrections and riots outside the Windsor and Rutland County Courts; in some cases, they involved hundreds of men. The insurgents protested land grant taxes and conditions at a time when people were having a hard time getting their feet on the ground. One account referred to the attorneys as pickpockets. In one case, Sheriffs Isaac "Rifle" Clark, Stephen Pearl and others were called to raise a militia with three days of provisions to combat the insurgents in southern Vermont. High Sheriff Benjamin Wait, another Green Mountain Boy, was called and ordered to find deputies and disperse a crowd of thirty or forty in Hartland. In a brief skirmish with bayonets, rifle stocks and clubs, twenty-seven insurgents were jailed.[139]

Meanwhile, it doesn't appear that civil unrest in the Champlain Islands ever approached the riot stage. Even if there had been uprisings, the county courthouse, which was the common protest site, would have been in Burlington, since, at that time, South Hero was in Chittenden County. It was later located in St. Albans, which was in Franklin County. The islands enjoyed a booming influx of people and growth, with a local economy that was self-supporting in many respects. Allen ran a store at his compound in South Hero. An October 10, 1788, a Two Heroes invoice to Allen's cousin Levi Allen itemized "3 fine handkerchiefs…3¾ yards of India Tafety" (silk) and one pair of women's staff shoes.[140]

In addition to his tavern, Allen ran a prosperous lumber business for a while, rafting lumber to Canada, which was a dangerous proposition at best. Cutting down enormous old-growth oak, maple, beech and pine trees before the invention of harvesters and forwarders, much less chainsaws, was not easy. The tools of the trade were axes and feller saws, which were large two-man handsaws. The trees needed to be limbed and cut to nominal lengths before they could be dragged out with oxen. If that wasn't demanding and dangerous enough, once the logs were on the lake, they had to be assembled into a huge log raft. The raft would be equipped with tents or shacks, a sail and oars. The rafts were subject to unpredictable weather, big waves on the lake, currents on the rivers and shoals, not to mention hostile encounters on the long, tedious journey. At that time, Ebenezer sent an invoice to Ira Allen for cutting and shipping 150,000 feet of white pine lumber to Quebec. The sawmills at Winooski

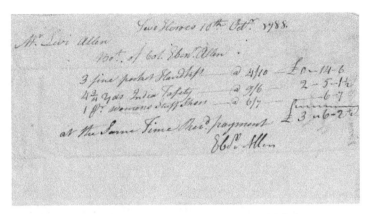

A 1788 Ebenezer Allen invoice to Levi Allen. *Courtesy of UVM Special Collections.*

Falls, Swanton Falls and Milton Falls were not built until the end of the eighteenth century. Logging involved a crew of "the hardest type of men," according to historian Ben Hall.[141]

In 1786, Allen was chosen as the second selectman for the newly named town of South Hero, and he was also elected as a representative to the Vermont General Assembly. He was reelected for many years, until 1798, and he continued to serve as the town clerk until 1795. He also continued to serve as a militia commander and problem solver for the young state of Vermont.

THE MISSISQUOI BAY INTRUDERS

In 1786, Governor Chittenden appointed Colonel Allen to remove all "unlawful intruders" in the Missisquoi Bay area by force. Who were the intruders?

It is well documented that the Abenaki had lived in the Vermont region, including Swanton, for thousands of years. Swanton had been chartered in 1763, and in 1765, the Abenakis had leased their lands on the bay to James Robertson of St. John, Quebec. When the Revolution began, many of the Abenakis left the Missisquoi area and headed north of the Canadian border to get out of harm's way. They later returned

A carved totem pole of Abenaki Chief Greylock, sitting in Battery Park, Burlington. Greylock lived in Swanton in the 1730s. *Photograph by the author.*

to the Missisquoi and found their villages gone and replaced with a growing population of White settlements. As a result, they threatened to dispossess the settlers. After a couple of raids, the Republic of Vermont got involved.

Ira Allen owned over 90 percent of Swanton as of 1786. His argument for the removal of the Abenaki from their unceded land held that the Natives were really from the St. Francis tribe in Canada and, furthermore, that any of the original inhabitants had lost their title as a consequence of the war with the French. He argued that, perhaps, they could find justice by applying to the courts of Vermont. This controversy is a whole other story that deserves further discussion at another time.[142]

As a result of the governor's orders, a small detachment of troops remained in the Missisquoi Bay area for at least two years to end the attacks and protect the settlers. We don't know how much force or negotiations were used to settle the conflict in Swanton. We do know, however, that tribal lands have continued to be in dispute over the ensuing centuries. Recently, in 2020, four Native tribes, including the Abenakis, were granted free fishing rights in Vermont after more than two hundred years.

THE UNCOMMON YEAR OF STARVATION

The summer of 1788 brought a severe drought; in fact, it was commonly called "the scarce year" and "the uncommon year of starvation." According to Zadock Thompson, Vermonters resorted to eating tadpoles at this time. Thompson also notes that dysentery was "universal" in Vermont during that time. The postwar economy was in terrible shape, and people were generally poor, living close to the land. Many families were starving and had a hard time surviving, especially in a region with a brutal winter climate. Ethan Allen's hay crop near the Winooski River in Burlington was depleted by February.[143]

Ebenezer Allen was more fortunate on the island, a few miles away as the crow flies, and Ebenezer would be remembered by what was about to transpire. Colonel Allen offered hay to General Ethan, and by the time Ethan Allen showed up at the Two Heroes Inn and Tavern with his hay wagon sleigh, Ebenezer had invited a number of the Green Mountain Boys over for an evening of storytelling with stonewalls and flips. Apparently, quite a crew showed up at Ebenezer's tavern to pay their respects to General Allen, the hero of Ticonderoga and the author of a best-selling book about his three-year captivity.

The group swapped old war stories, and some drank into the wee hours. After some socializing, fifty-two-year-old Ethan Allen retired relatively early and woke before daybreak to head back on the short trip across the ice with his hired man on his loaded hay wagon. Ethan suffered a traumatic medical event during the return trip, probably a stroke, and never regained consciousness. Although he was treated with bloodletting by a well-meaning acquaintance, he passed away in his bed a few days later. He was subsequently celebrated with a large funeral at his brother Ira's place in Winooski; from there, he was carried across the ice on the river to Burlington and up the hill to Greenmount Cemetery, where he was buried after men chopped a grave into the frozen February soil.

Later in that same uncommon year of starvation, two citizens were brought before Justice of the Peace Allen after it was proven that they had stolen food to eat. One man was apparently quite affluent. Colonel Allen expressed "great chagrin" at the thieves and noted that scarcity could be no excuse for stealing. After ruling against the prisoners, their counsel countered that the arrest warrant had not been signed and, therefore, the whole proceeding should have been legally nullified. According to Allen's grandson Dr. Barnes, Allen took the summons, signed it and then said, "Now, go to trial. Everybody knows I'm Justice itself!"[144]

Colonel Allen lived in South Hero for another decade. In 1790, South Hero was the most populated town in northern Vermont, with over 1,000 inhabitants. As a point of reference, Burlington only had a population of 332 in the 1790 census. But Allen wasn't content to retire, kick back and rest. He was driven to find new opportunities and continued to be active in his side hustles. For almost a year, in 1792–93, Ebenezer toured unsettled territories with a group of investors that was led by his namesake, the Loyalist Ebenezer Allen, who had also fought at the Battle of Bennington, but for the British side. The group, including Allen's cousin and high-roller Ira Allen, toured western New York, Ohio and the Niagara regions in search of land speculation opportunities.

THE ROYAL SPECTACLE ON ALLEN'S POINT

In February 1793, a distinguished entourage of royal British travelers stayed as guests at Allen's inn. They included twenty-six-year-old Prince Edward Augustus, Duke of Kent and Strathearn, and his mistress, Madame Alphonsine-Thérèse-Bernardine-Julie de Montgenêt de Saint-Laurent. They arrived at Allen's inn while en route from their home in Quebec City, and they had plans to travel to Boston and New York City. The duke's father, His Excellency King George III, had banished the prince to Quebec City in 1791, after he became aware of his illicit relationship with the Madame de Saint-Laurent, who was not from an appropriate social class. Followers of the eighteenth-century British royal family know that Prince Edward was the king's fourth son of fifteen children. In 1819, Prince Edward became the father of Queen Victoria, his only child.[145]

Madame de Saint-Laurent arrived elegantly attired and covered in several fur robes on one of a handful of sleighs. She was a widow who happened to be seven years older than the duke. Although she did not have royal status, by several accounts, she was beautiful, clever, witty and managed the Duke's household with propriety and dignity. In fact, Governor Benning, a personal friend of the prince and Madame, was evidently quite enamored with her charms. It should be noted that Prince Edward was not married at the time and had a long-term relationship with his so-called mistress before he married and settled down with another woman and became a father.

The duke's sleighs were impressive, but they were nothing compared to King George's eight-ton, twenty-four-foot-long, thirteen-foot-tall gilded carriage. Nonetheless, the crop-eared horses, four officers and enormous sleighs were conspicuous to any who witnessed them on the rustic windswept island landscape in northern Vermont. Each sleigh was pulled by a couple of teams of beautiful horses and accompanied by military security guards on horseback. The duke's valets unloaded at least twenty carryall trunks from the sleighs. The entourage included two aides, two bodyguards, a cook and the Madame's large dog.[146]

Although the Two Heroes Inn was not as posh as the accommodations the royal visitors were accustomed to, they enjoyed Allen's tour of the island and his hospitality. The prince's cook prepared the provisions, which they had brought with them. Madame de Saint-Laurent was congenial and more proper than some of the inn's usual guests. The duke conversed with his "lady" in French and treated her very kindly. The two bodyguards slept by

Left: Prince Edward Augustus, the Duke of Kent, who was the fourth son of King George III of Britain. *Public domain*.

Right: Prince Edward's only child, Victoria, who became Queen Victoria. *Public domain*.

the prince's door. But the trip from Quebec City to Burlington wouldn't happen without some Vermont excitement and a near disaster.

After staying at the Two Heroes Inn, the royal entourage headed across the ice of Mallets Bay to Burlington to stay for a couple of nights at the home of Horace Loomis, a highly respected gentleman who was in the leather business. Between Allen's Point and the Colchester-Burlington shoreline, according to author Mollie Gillen, "The Prince had the shock and mortification of seeing two of the sleighs carrying 'the whole of his baggage, consisting of what plate, linen, clothes, &c, he then possessed,' fall through the cracking surface into the lake."[147] We don't know if horses or sleighs were lost, but apparently, the prince's wardrobe and no doubt much more was swallowed up by the lake and now lie somewhere in the depths of the bay. The prince apparently purchased new haberdasheries after reaching Boston.

Loomis was one of the prominent early landowners with one hundred beautiful acres of partially cleared forest in the "quality" hill section part of Burlington. When the entourage departed Burlington, Madame de Saint-Laurent was headed to New York to visit a friend, and the Prince

Madame Alphonsine-Thérèse-Bernardine-Julie de Montgenêt de Saint-Laurent, also known as Madame de Saint-Laurent, was the partner of Prince Edward for twenty-seven years. *Public domain.*

was going by a separate route to Boston. They had plans to rendezvous later on for some fun in the sun in the West Indies.

Prince Edward was friends with Henry Knox and other high rollers in Boston, Philadelphia and New York City. A flurry of social activities ensued when the prince finally cruised into Boston after the fifteen-day journey that had begun on January 22. Several funny Vermont stories followed the prince and spread along the way. One story concerned the landlady of a tavern who commented that the Bible was a favorite book (of Americans), but when they wanted amusement, Americans would read Peter Pindar. Pindar was the pen name of John Wolcot, a British satirist. And for that, the prince thought she was "dumb as an oyster." Another anecdote related that someone asked an outraged man how he felt about his wife being kissed by the prince. The man's answer was, "How does it make the prince feel to get his butt kicked by a tailor?"[148]

A third story sounds remarkably similar to the kind of thing one of the Allens or their close associates might have said to the prince, and apparently, it tickled all of Boston. The dialogue between the prince and a plain Vermont farmer went like this:

> At a tavern, an honest New England man thus accosts him—"Well, how do you do, sir, and are you really the Son of King George?"
>
> He answered that he was, "Amazing!" said the man. "And how does your daddy do?"
>
> "He was well," said the Prince, "when I heard last from him."
>
> "Well, now," said the honest man, "don't you thing [sic] he was wrong in quarrelling with America as he did?"
>
> "I don't know, but he was," said the other. "But there is no forseeing, at all times, how matters will turn out."
>
> "True," said the man. "But if it had'nt [sic] been for that plaguy Quarrell, I suppose he might have been king here yet!"[149]

These stories remind us that humor has always been prevalent, and even in the eighteenth century, class differences offered good stock to serve as a foundation of humor. And, even though Colonel Allen was a hardscrabble self-made frontiersman, he was prominent enough to rub elbows with the upper echelons of global power and money.

THE COMPANY WE KEEP

On the last day of January 1795, Allen sat in the darkly lit Ames Tavern after a few stonewalls, catching up with other local legends. The tavern sat on the main stage road between Castleton and Montreal in Burlington, near

Ames Tavern, at 411 Colchester Avenue in Burlington, as it is seen today. The tavern was within sight of Ira Allen's blockhouse, home and mills on the Onion River. *Photograph by the author.*

the Onion River. The Ames Tavern owners knew him as Colonel Allen, the fabled war hero, Green Mountain Boy and fellow tavern keeper. He sat in the shadows of smoky candlelight, squinting over a piece of paper and scrawling a note with a quill pen.

The letter was written to his cousin "General Ira Allen," whose headquarters was only a quarter mile away, just across the Onion (Winooski) River. Since it was the end of January, the river ferry wasn't running, nor was the river frozen thick enough to chance a walk across. Ames Tavern was yet another Burlington tavern that had just been established in 1795 by Thomas Ames. The colonial building with a huge central brick chimney and several fireplaces still remains standing today, 228 years later, at 411 Colchester Avenue. At the time, several other taverns, breweries and distilleries dotted the business district in the town, which was closer to the lake.

In his letter, Allen asked for some business advice and bantered some suggestive colloquy that may have been referring to an ongoing dispute with Sheriff Stephen Pearl. This dispute would shortly turn into a civil lawsuit, as we shall see. Allen may have been concerned with the wisdom of leaving town at a time when he was likely to become a defendant in a trial. During the 1795 trip, in a note to Ira, Ebenezer reported from Canada that they were traveling on horseback through two-foot-deep snow, near the Niagara River. He requested that Ira send Captain John Martin, who would be helpful in translating Mohawk language.[150]

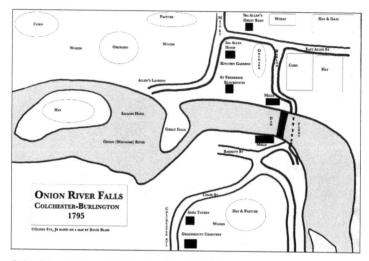

Onion (Winooski) River, 1795, the site of Ira Allen's blockhouse, home and mills. Ames Tavern was located at the site labeled "Woods" in the bottom center. *Image by the author.*

Of course, over the long term, Ebenezer kept his nose to the grindstone, worked multiple side hustles, resisted taking on credit, balanced his books and left a robust estate. In comparison, Ira Allen overleveraged everything he could and acquired land until he eventually lost his shirt and escaped imprisonment for unpaid debt by moving to Philadelphia, where he died a pauper. So, it appears that, in the end, Ebenezer did okay with or without his high-rolling cousin's advice.

Allen was also familiar with the luminary Mohawk military and political leader Joseph Brant from western New York State, who was personally acquainted with both General Washington and King George III. Brant had followers who lived on nearby Stave Island, near Allen's Point on Lake Champlain, and they used to visit Allen on occasion.

Brant was a gifted, colorful, well-educated and, in some ways, entitled Mohawk warrior-leader who had fought with the Loyalists during the Revolution in Oswego County, New York, and Pennsylvania. By 1795, Brant was disenfranchised with the British, as they refused to support the Natives after signing the Treaty of Paris with the American colonies in 1783. He and Allen were born in the same year; both were charismatic military leaders, and by that time, both were trying to live with the ambiguity of the aftermath that followed war.

The friendly Natives, who Melvin Barnes identified as Brant followers, traveled with Allen out to the Midwest during the 1795 adventure. The entourage also included Vermonters Charles Whitney and Robert Randal, as well as "Englanders" John Askin and William Robertson. The Michigan State Archives explain how the businessmen had planned to "extinguish the Indian title" and buy 20 million acres of land on the Michigan Lower Peninsula from the U.S. government for $500,000. Allen's group had created a stock company, and Whitney and Randall promised several Congressmen stock or cash for support of the plan. The scheme was exposed, Whitney and Randall were investigated by the U.S. House and the plan quickly fell apart.[151]

This affair might have been a case in point of Melvin Barnes's comment that Allen was sometimes easily talked into schemes that were not in his best interest by less scrupulous individuals. Despite Allen's infatuation with the greener pastures of the Midwest, his family dissuaded him from moving out to the Michigan area. Today, the Lower Peninsula of Michigan is still largely forested with plenty of rural farmland, two hundred years later.

Barnes noted that once he returned from that trip, Allen fully enjoyed his family and friends, hospitality, favorite politicians, horses, dogs and impressive farm. But another shadow was cast in Barnes's biography of Allen.

THE QUESTION OF INDICTMENTS FOR MURDER

Dr. Melvin Barnes wrote in Allen's short biography that, in 1798, Colonel Ebenezer Allen, in his capacity as a Franklin County sheriff, made the arrest of a man named John Gregg from Alburgh, Vermont, who died in his custody. This story involved Allen tracking down and arresting a wanted American man in Canada. By a tragic twist of fate, the prisoner drowned in the lake before he could be returned to be incarcerated.

As clear cut as Barnes's story sounds, Ebenezer Allen's involvement in this affair is nowhere to be found in the public records; in fact, there is no record of Allen ever being the sheriff for Chittenden, Grand Isle or Franklin Counties. When researching and tracing back the primary sources, we don't really have a clear explanation of exactly who was involved aside from the victim, John Griggs. According to the records of the governor and the

Vermont assembly, Governor Isaac Tichenor spoke to the "occurrence of so serious and delicate nature" and addressed the Vermont assembly on October 19, 1799. Tichenor said he had received official communication from Canada pertaining to the death of John Gregg. Isaac Tichenor had served on the Vermont Supreme Court, was elected to serve as governor for twelve years and served as a U.S. senator for six years. He was known for his fine manners, loquacious eloquence and dapper appearance. In fact, he was fondly known as "Jersey Slick."[152]

Tichenor said Gregg had drowned in Lake Champlain while in the custody of "certain

Governor Issac Tichenor. *Courtesy of the Vermont Historical Society.*

citizens of this state, who had inconsiderately arrested the deceased within the territory of his Britannic Majesty. Bills of indictment charging these citizens with the murder of said Gregg, were found in the Colonial Court of King's Bench of Criminal Jurisdiction in Montreal, and a demand to deliver over these citizens for trial was made."[153]

Unexpectedly, there was no John Gregg listed as a landowner in the Alburgh town records of 1798. In fact, there are no Greggs listed in the Alburgh town records index. There is, however, a man named John Griggs who lived in Alburgh from 1780 to 1798. This is the same John Griggs who was confronted on his lot allegedly by Colonel Allen's posse back in 1781.

The *Alburgh Land Records* include a 1796 entry that shows Griggs defaulted on the purchase of several lots and reneged on an agreement of a payment plan to a man named Reuben Taylor. Griggs owed Taylor several thousand dollars. The unusual entry on page 59 of the *Alburgh Land Records* amounts to a warrant for Griggs's arrest and "safe return" so he could appear in county court. Further, based on documents in the land records that show Griggs was still alive in June 1798, we can narrow down his death in 1798 to December of that year, since the lake doesn't freeze until December. The records of the Vermont assembly confirm the story of "Griggs" (not "Gregg") dying in the custody of a deputy sheriff of Franklin County by the name of John Allen, not Ebenezer Allen.

The Vermont assembly's account of the tragedy goes like this: Griggs had fled to hide at his brother's home a short distance from the Vermont–Canada border. Deputy Sheriff John Allen from St. Albans, Vermont, along with a posse, tracked Griggs down, broke into his room and arrested him. They bound Griggs and put him on a sleigh to take him back to Vermont. While in Allen's custody, on the way around the point called "the tongue" of Alburgh, south of the Canada–Vermont border, the sleigh went through the ice. Griggs drowned in Lake Champlain. Keep in mind that Governor Tichenor, Governor Chittenden, Udney Hay and many other assemblymen were original grantees in the towns of South Hero, Alburgh and North Hero, near Allen's residence in South Hero. Ebenezer Allen was also serving in the Vermont assembly until 1798. He was a household name in Vermont.

A subsequent court of inquiry that was held in Alburgh investigated the incident in May 1799, and it concluded that Griggs "was legally liable for arrest" and that the drowning was accidental. Vermont assemblymen Udney Hay, Jonathan Robinson and Reverend Asa Lyon, himself a celebrated resident of Alburg, served on a committee to prepare a report and resolution for the house.

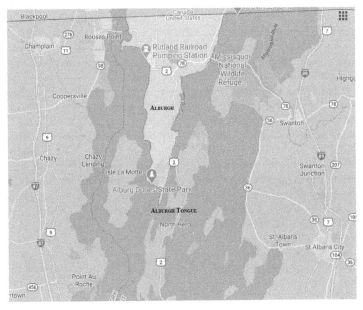

A map showing the Canadian border at the top and Alburgh Tongue near the center, where John Griggs met his fate. *Courtesy of Google Maps.*

VERMONT'S EBENEZER ALLEN

This story is a conspiracy theorist's gold mine. It would seem odd that Ebenezer Allen's grandson would confuse a murder investigation of a deputy sheriff from St. Albans named John Allen with that of his grandfather Colonel Ebenezer Allen from South Hero. Is it possible that Ebenezer was part of the posse with Deputy Sheriff John Allen? Or is it possible that he was the sheriff and Deputy John Allen took the heat for him? Ebenezer would have been fifty-five by 1798. Is it possible that Barnes, being only four or five years old at the time of the incident, misinterpreted old stories and rumors or the identity of the responsible sheriff? If Colonel Allen was involved, did being a multiterm Vermont legislator who was serving in 1798 offer some impunity? If that was the case, would the legislature have gone so far as to conceal Allen's involvement and whitewash the books? Why would an educated, articulate man such as Governor Tichenor repeatedly misspeak of John Griggs as John Gregg? Why did the governor not mention the "certain persons" who were accused by name? Were personnel matters in 1798 shielded from the press in the same way they sometimes are today?

Alburgh is part of the island community, and the "assistants" in Deputy John Allen's posse might have been part of the island community. Each of the surviving posse members would have known exactly who was involved and what the circumstances were. They would have needed to live with and manage that information. At this point, further details and characters remain unknown, but we know that a man named Prince B. Hall was the St. Albans sheriff at the time. And we know that Enos Wood was serving as a deputy. Maybe with time, we will uncover more names of the men who were in the posse and learn more about this mysterious case.

Regardless of whether Ebenezer Allen was involved or not, we cannot help but wonder about the public sentiment in the Champlain Islands in the wake of this incident. In all likelihood, the community would have been embroiled in highly charged gossip about Griggs and the posse with grief, drama, indictments and weeks of investigation. The conjecture and rumors must have weighed heavily on everyone. Regardless of whether or not Colonel Allen was involved, we can presume that this event and its aftermath may have had an impact on what happened next. Whatever the reason, Allen needed a change of scenery.

A CHANGE OF SCENERY

The town of Burlington was still a densely wooded hillside with some cleared farms by the turn of the century. The lake lapped the shoreline below Water Street, now Battery Street, during high water in the spring. A thriving lumber shipping mecca was rooting on the bayside waterfront. The growing population of nine hundred inhabitants was growing by leaps and bounds and mostly comprised farm families on one-hundred-acre lots and smaller subdivided lots in the center; these lots then spread out from the Winooski River to the boundary of Shelburne on the south end of town.

Livestock grazed everywhere, as they were without enough fences, boundaries or an animal pound for strays. In fact, so many cows and pigs roamed the streets that the town employed haywards, or officers in charge of cattle fences. Despite the inconveniences of keeping so many animals, including the corresponding trails of effluvium, the town residents voted again and again, from 1793 until 1804, to allow swine to roam the streets. One of the few requirements was that hogs should be "well rung in the nose, with a good and sufficient ring" and "well yoaked" with wood, which could be grabbed if necessary. They also required that the yoke be worn eight inches above the neck and four inches below the bar.[154]

Burlington never lacked for lodging and human watering holes either. By 1800, a man named Daniel Staniford owned a distillery on the north side of Pearl Street, near the present Winooski Avenue. Staniford brewed ale, beer and porter and gin.[155] Other establishments, such as Jesse Hollister's and Gideon King's, served customers on the waterfront, and Ames Tavern served the other side of town, close to the Onion River.

In 1800, Allen moved to the booming town of Burlington and opened his own tavern at the foot of the wharf on the south wharf, by the bay. On the 1830 Burlington map, the south wharf is located at the bottom left of the image. A brewery is labeled on the map at the bottom of Wharf Street, which is now Maple Street. We don't know exactly where Allen's tavern was, and the buildings from the late 1700s near the waterfront are long gone, but it is plausible it was at or near or at the brewery location, approximately where Waterfront Diving Center exists today. Based on Burlington land deeds, two years after Allen's death, his wife, Lydia, sold one acre and one shop to their son Timothy Allen for fifty dollars.

None of the buildings from that time exist in the city today, although several brick and stone structures exist there that were built in the 1830s. But by then, a horse story had caught up with Allen. In fact, he was apparently imprisoned after being sued in a civil suit by his friend Sheriff Stephen Pearl in 1797.[156] The first courthouse in Burlington had been built in 1795 on what was then called Courthouse Square, which was located in what is now the center of City Hall Park. The jail was a sturdy log

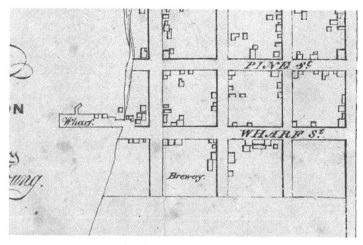

A map of the intersection of Wharf Street (now Maple Street and Battery Street, the location of Allen's Tavern from 1800 to 1806). *Courtesy of UVM Special Collections.*

building, complete with an outdoor whipping post for punishing convicted criminals. Another account says a second courthouse was built in the same location in 1802, and a pine tree out front served as the whipping post.[157]

Piecing together the circumstances of the lawsuit was difficult; however, Allen's motives are even more puzzling. Colonel Pearl was a few years younger than Allen and of a similar pedigree. He was also a war veteran and public servant who had been granted land, and he lived on Grand Isle (then a part of Chittenden County). They both had been employed as sheriffs, justices of the peace and select board members during the 1780s and 1790s in South Hero. Both men had moved to Burlington. Pearl had large land holdings around the same time as Allen and was also known to speculate in real estate. According to genealogical records, Pearl was involved in a number of land trades and sales. And by some accounts, he was as lovable as a teddy bear. G.B. Sawyer, Esq., said:

> *Col. Pearl was a large and portly man, and although rather clumsy, had a fine and imposing presence, a genial and benevolent look, and a courtly and unfaltering manner in any company, and under all circumstances.... There never was another such a man. He had such an extraordinary power to please, he commanded and charmed men, women and children. His great characteristics were sense, wit and benevolence. An old friend could never pass by his door unhailed. We united conspicuously majesty and beauty of form and countenance, and as he stood in his porch, his tall, large, magnificent form looked like a colossus. He was a large and beneficent landholder, with that wonderful tact of distribution, that while his divisions made others rich, they did not impoverish him. He was a captain at Bunker Hill, and a major (I think) when he came out of the Revolution.... The records of Burlington show that while he was town clerk, he labeled the town records "Stephen Pearl's Book of Truth."*[158]

By all accounts, Pearl was a well-respected and accomplished leader in Burlington and served as a tax collector and in other capacities for many years. It is difficult to psychoanalyze the interpersonal dynamic between Allen and Pearl, but we do know that they both had big personalities and egos. Looking at the court records of the lawsuit, through the 220 years with different legal procedures, handwriting analysis of the records, convoluted legal terminology and explanations, the abridged version of the story is something like this.

In 1793, Deputy Sheriff Enos Wood of North Hero (Allen's original fellow Two Heroes Island founder), confiscated two red mares and a cow from Nathaniel Wate of North Hero on a legal warrant. The horses apparently were going to go to John Staniford as part of a legal settlement. They were eventually going to be returned to Staniford. For whatever reason, Deputy Wood gave the two horses to Colonel Allen in South Hero and received a written receipt from Allen in return. Allen was to return the "goods and chattel" to Sheriff Pearl. However, for whatever reason, Colonel Allen decided not to surrender the horses and the cow. When Sheriff Pearl attempted to recover the animals so that they could be returned to their rightful owner, John Staniford, he was denied by Colonel Allen.[159]

After having promised to return the animals to Sheriff Pearl, Allen insisted on keeping the animals. Hence, Pearl sued Allen in an attempt to recover damages for the animals and the court. The original trial was held in 1797. In 1800, Allen appealed the verdict, and again, the court sided with Sheriff Pearl. After Allen's attorneys managed to appeal to the Vermont legislature, which Allen knew well, on a technicality, the legislature relented and ruled that Allen should get a new trial. Both men "lawyered up" again with multiple attorneys. Allen stood trial once more, and ultimately, in 1803, he lost the judgment to the plaintiff, Sheriff Pearl. The jury ruled against the defendant, Allen, and he paid $129 in damages.[160]

From this vantage point, it seems like there might have been more to the story. The 1800 journal of the general assembly recorded that Ebenezer contended, in 1793, that he never received a delivery of the cow and horses. Maybe this was the case; otherwise, the persistent behavior from Colonel Allen doesn't add up. But if that was true, why did Pearl prevail and Allen get fined? Did Allen give away the beautiful horses to the legendary celebrity Joseph Brant, or did he give them to someone else? Perhaps someone owed Allen a debt and keeping the horses was his way of settling the score. It is unfortunate that this is the extent of the paper trail that was left behind by Allen's six-year tenure in Burlington.

As far as we know, Allen continued running his tavern business in Burlington, although there is no direct reference to his tavern found in an exhaustive search of letters, journals and literature. Since currency was scarce and speculators often leveraged their land or promissory notes for products and services, personal debt was at an epidemic level. Men who were sued for their failure to pay debts were commonly imprisoned in the town jail. When the jail overflowed, the town contracted with taverns

Ebenezer Allen's grave in Elmwood Cemetery in Burlington, Vermont, which is visible from the sidewalk on Elmwood Avenue. *Photograph by the author.*

to house debtors, and in Burlington, debtors were notably housed at Jesse Hollister's and Gideon King's Taverns' debtors' rooms. In fact, Allen's cousin Levi Allen, who was around Allen's age, died in debtor's captivity at the jail or King's Tavern in 1801. Thankfully, this would not be Ebenezer's fate, as he left a healthy estate to his heirs.

Colonel Allen passed away on March 26, 1806, at the old age of sixty-three. He was given the honor of a Masonic service and interment in Burlington. A funeral march proceeded from Burlington's Washington Lodge to Allen's home, and his casket was brought to the courthouse for the large funeral. He was eulogized as a benevolent, honest Patriot and "the noblest work of God."[161] Allen's remains were buried in Elmwood Cemetery in Burlington. His Baroque tripartite headstone is inscribed erroneously with a death date of 1807. It is adorned by an American veteran flag. Shortly after Allen's death, Lydia Allen returned to South Hero and lived with their son Timothy on Allen's Point. Timothy eventually moved to Constable, New York. Lydia passed away in 1833 at the age of eighty-eight.

Epilogue

Writing an authentic biography about a man who was born 277 years ago, before Vermont was settled with European colonists and without much of his own recorded history is a challenge. As one of Allen's neighbors said, the only mode of communication was by canoe. Typeset printers were few and far between in the New Hampshire Land Grants. Only the timely written word could be trusted for accurate history, and even that was subject to the filters of the storyteller.

Fortunately, in 1853, a brief biography—however metaphorically interpretive—of Ebenezer Allen was published by his grandson Dr. Melvin Barnes Jr. That booklet summarized the life of a man who Barnes believed merited "much of the recognition so liberally accorded his contemporaries." The fact that his biography was written at all, much less forty-four years after his death, suggests the belief that, although Allen lived in a generation of heroes, he left an imprint, despite leaving virtually no paper trail. Nonetheless, his deeds far outpaced and outweighed many of his contemporaries.

Despite the lack of breadcrumbs, scrapbooks, diaries or details from Ebenezer's life, today, we have the luxury of genealogy websites, town histories, gazetteers, journals, pension affidavits, archives, museums, family letters and special collections that have been left behind for humanity to treasure. Weaving together a legitimate portrait of this hero on a small stage reveals a man who exemplified the true character of invincible patriotism and hardworking American grit. We also find a man who possessed some faith in a higher entity and a conviction in virtues. With that spirit, he generously gave what he had to offer to ambitiously carve out and build a republic.

Human lives are defined by the era in which they live, and that era puts everything they become into context. Allen's era was a time of unceded Native land, rampant diseases, political and religious upheaval and bloody barbaric warfare, all while building a foundation for a new democracy before there were new laws and order. Many of the diseases were befuddling and often fatal with pre–germ theory medicine. There is only one mention of Allen being very ill on returning home from getting provisions in 1783, but otherwise, aside from losing an infant, his family seemed to avoid deaths and disability from smallpox, influenza, tuberculosis and injuries during a violent era with multiple enemies. It is easy to see why colonial settlers put so much faith in God; there was very little faith to be found in science, medicine and their enemies.

We don't find hard evidence of Allen drinking heavily, but that is not to say he was a teetotaler. During the American Revolution, alcohol was practically considered its own food group. It was commonly used as medicine for just about everything, no matter how absurd that contradicts the research of today. It wasn't until 1814 that Dr. James Mann stated that he believed alcohol increased the risk of disease and death in his patients in Burlington, Vermont. We know now that alcohol abuse increases the risks of physiological and mental health issues. However, even though it is inconclusive if Allen drank as much as some of the other Green Mountain Boys, he did learn the benefits of owning and running a tavern at a time when there was plenty of money to be made in that line of work. Given his celebrity status and popularity, it is easy to see how his establishment would have been a popular gathering place.

Hearing the personal accounts of the terrors of war with slow-loading rifles, cannon loads raking devastating artillery fire and hand-to-hand combat with swords and bayonets is a reminder of the trauma and stress that the survivors carried with them for the rest of their lives. Nowadays, we know that living through violent experiences with extreme stress and the physical, mental and emotional tolls of battle comes at a cost; it can leave deep psychological scars. Close-combat situations, fighting the enemy face to face, was a different experience than shooting from a distance, which is more prevalent in modern battles.

Not much was written about post-traumatic stress disorder during the American Revolution, but we can assume it was present. Psychology hadn't been discovered by 1777, and it would be years before studying the health of the mind came into fashion. When considering the American Revolution, we shouldn't forget that the veterans and, in some cases, the non-veterans were exposed to terror and atrocities that would have left an impact on them and their families. One must wonder about the toll of the continual claps of thunder, the trauma of battle, the untold injuries, the tens of thousands of miles on horseback and marching in shoes that bear no comparison to the comfortable gear we have today.

In reflecting on his grandfather, Dr. Melvin Barnes Jr. stated that, through most of his adult life, Allen had been surrounded by enemies and mountains, and when he moved to the Champlain Islands during the 1780s, for the first time in his life, he was surrounded only by water. Perhaps this alluded to the stresses of extended episodes of violence, grief, physical endurance and survival he had witnessed. Perhaps we should take into account the inherent traumas that faced men, women and children during the American Revolution.

From all accounts, we are left with combat scenarios that depict an invincible Allen as a larger-than-life character with a knack for strategy and deliberate action that, in some cases, seemed to defy the odds and imply divine providence. We know from the Barnes biography that Lydia Allen and their children escaped raids and attacks by running and hiding. How did Allen escape battle wounds, diseases or worse when at least two of his commanders, Colonel Potter and Colonel Brown, had both either died or been killed in action by 1780? Could Allen have been savvy enough to avoid situations that were too risky? He certainly engaged in some high-risk attacks in fierce combat, so it would not seem likely that he shied away from danger. But perhaps he had a knack for reading situations that others could not. Maybe his multilingual proficiency helped him through some potential scrapes with Natives. The following is a case in which language proficiency made all the difference.

In his biography, Ira Allen described how he, Remember Baker and a "Dutchman" named Van Ornam drove off a dozen or so Natives who were accompanying some Yorker surveyors on the Onion River in 1772. Fortunately, Van Ornam had had the good fortune of having been a prisoner in the captivity of Natives. While in captivity, he had learned some of the Native language. During Ira Allen's tense standoff on the river, Van Ornam told the Natives in their own language that the conflict was a land dispute between the Americans and British that didn't concern them. He added they were welcome to hunt on the lands whenever they wanted. The Natives promptly left, and the small party of Yorker surveyors left as well after Ira Allen promised to kill them if they returned.

Perhaps Ebenezer Allen's Teflon-coated invincible charisma played a role in keeping him safe. And maybe he had guardian angels guiding and watching over him. Or maybe a combination of these factors helped him thrive and survive through the war with relative impunity.

When a leader is always ready to take it to the next level, shows unwavering confidence in himself and the men in his unit and executes deliberate brazen actions to subdue the enemy, unusual and great things happen. This is the hallmark of proficiency and mastery of a craft. When he does it repeatedly, he becomes an omnipotent hero in military circles and a legend in life. And once he becomes a legend, he has power, earned respect and political capital.

Several unanswered questions remain from Allen's story. What became of Dinah and Nancy Mattis? Was Allen involved in the John Griggs's ordeal in Alburgh? What was his rationale for not returning the horses to Sheriff Pearl in the civil lawsuit? What were his last six years like in Burlington? What caused his death?

As we uncover more evidence, further clues may emerge to identify who was on the posse and what role Colonel Allen played, if any, in the death of Griggs. We may eventually be able to explain Allen's decision that triggered the Pearl lawsuit. Although both Timothy and Allen's widow, Lydia, sold the Allen property after his death, Ebenezer Allen's name doesn't come up on any town of Burlington land records deeds between 1798, when they began recording land deeds, and 1808, after he passed away. Was this evidence of shrewd business practice to underexpose his risk to creditors and put the deeds in Lydia's name, or was there another reason for this?

For now, we close this chapter on an extraordinary early American Patriot, commando and emancipator. Hopefully, this biography will help renew interest in Allen and inspire deeper research to answer these questions and more.

Chart 1

Ebenezer Allen's Parents, Siblings and Children

Parents	Siblings	Children
Samuel Allen 1705–1755	Waity Allen Rice 1732–1816	
Hannah Miller 1707–1771	Noah Allen 1734–1822	Abiel Allen 1763–1765
	Jemima Allen 1736–?	
	Samuel Allen 1740–1801	Timothy Allen 1765–1850
	Ebenezer Allen 1743–1806	Mary Allen 1766–?
	Samuel Allen 1740–1801	Charlotte E. Barnes 1767–1813
	Rachel Allen 1747–?	Lydia Martin 1768–1813
	Seth Allen 1750–1777	Ebenezer W. Allen 1771–1844
	Hannah Allen Coy 1753–1837	Vashti Palmer 1774–1840
Zebulon Richards 1718–1800 Lydia Brown 1718–?	**Lydia (Richards) Allen** 1746–1833	Amy Boardman 1775/1781–1813
		Eunice Luther 1779–1852

Wikitree. "Family Tree & Genealogy Tools for Ebenezer Allen JP." www.wikitree.com.
Geni. "Colonel Ebenezer Allen." www.geni.com.

Chart 2

Ebenezer Allen–Ethan Allen
Genealogy

Samuel Allen 1
Windsor, CT
1588–1648

Samuel Allen 2	Nehemiah Allen 2
1634–1719	?–1684
↓	↓
Samuel Allen 3	Samuel Allen 3
1675–1739	1665/1666–1718
↓	↓
Samuel Allen 4	Joseph Allen 4
1706–1755	1708–1755
↓	↓
Ebenezer Allen 5	Ethan Allen 5
1743–1806	1737/1738–1789

Allen, Orrin P. "The Allen Memorial, Second Series, C.B. Fiske & Company, Palmer, Massachusetts, 1907." www.archive.org

Chart 3

THE GREEN MOUNTAIN BOYS, HERRICK'S RANGERS AND WARNER'S REGIMENT

M any of the original Green Mountain Boys enlisted in Herrick's Rangers militia and Warner's Colonial regiment. Both of these organizations were active, with different missions for different purposes. Warner's Regiment was equivalent to a national army—except there was no nation yet, so it was called a colonial regiment.

	Green Mountain Boys	Herrick's Rangers	Warner's Regiment
Who they were	A Bennington-based minuteman militia that was formed to rebel against New York sheriffs, Tories and others who were not sympathetic to the New Hampshire and, later, Vermont cause	An official Vermont Republic and state militia that was formed to take military action against British-led enemies of the cause of Vermont Territory and its people	The colonial regiment of up to five hundred men, established by the Continental Congress to defend the colonies from the British from 1775 to 1781

Chart 3

	Green Mountain Boys	Herrick's Rangers	Warner's Regiment
Size	Several hundred men	Three hundred men, many of the original Green Mountain Boys. Sometimes called the Green Mountain Boys	Up to a couple of hundred men, many of the original Green Mountain Boys
Pay	Folklore and gratitude	Paid by the colony of New Hampshire and Vermont	Paid by the colony of New York, since there was no national treasury or money in Vermont

Notes

Chapter 1

1. Barnes, *Short Biography*.
2. Minkema, "Defense," 23–59.
3. Kalif, "Blacksmithing."
4. Barnes, *Short Biography*.
5. Allen, *Allen Memorial*.

Chapter 2

6. Spencer, "Allen, Ethan."
7. Tice, "Epidemics and Pandemics."
8. American Academy of Pediatrics, "Diphtheria."
9. Robinson, "Timothy Allen."
10. Procknow, "Rebel and the Tory."
11. Smith, "Green Mountain Insurgency," 197.
12. Ibid.
13. Ashley, "Poultney."
14. Poultney Historical Society, "Colonial Times to Independence."
15. Reynolds, email to author, October 16, 2020.
16. Morabito, "Tithing Men."
17. Smith and Rann, eds., *History of Rutland County*, 822.

Chapter 3

18. Powers, "Ebenezer Allen."
19. Bascom and Holden, "Ticonderoga Expedition," 824.
20. Broom, "Ebenezer Allen," 3.
21. Bascom and Holden, "Ticonderoga Expedition," 826–28.
22. Philbrick, *Bunker Hill*.
23. Colonel Seth Warner's Extra-Continental Regiment, "Biography."
24. Broom, "Ebenezer Allen," 4.
25. Ibid.
26. Ibid.
27. Goodrich, *Rolls of the Soldiers*, 774.
28. Broom, "Ebenezer Allen," 4–5.
29. *Encyclopedia Americana*, 26.
30. Underwood, "Indian and Tory Raids,"
31. Broom, "Ebenezer Allen," 5–6.
32. Underwood, "Indian and Tory Raids," 205.
33. Ibid., 206.
34. Broom, "Ebenezer Allen," 5.
35. Hall, *Eastern Vermont*, 581.
36. Ibid.
37. Gauthier, email to the author, October 20, 2020.
38. Graham, "Siege."
39. Smith and Rann, eds., *History of Rutland County*, 733.
40. Caverly, *History of Pittsford*, 1, 2, 4.
41. Powers, phone interview with the author, October 27, 2020.
42. Underwood, "Indian and Tory Raids."
43. Ibid.

Chapter 4

44. Broom, "Ebenezer Allen, II," 5.
45. Nye, "Loyalists."
46. Broom, "Ebenezer Allen, II," 5.
47. Darling, *Red Coat*.
48. United States Army, *Ranger Handbook*, 1.
49. Thompson, *History*, 220.
50. Mullen, personal email communication with the author, November 4, 2020.
51. Barnes, *Short Biography*, 12.
52. Ibid., 13.
53. Ibid.

Chapter 5

54. Richmond, Vermont, "History."

55. Goodwin, "Narrative of the Captive."

56. Broom, "Ebenezer Allen," 6.

57. Goodrich, *Rolls of the Soldiers*.

58. Smith and Rann, eds., *History of Rutland County*, 824.

59. Ibid., 825.

60. Ibid.

61. Barnes, *Short Biography*, 12.

62. "Colonel Isaac Clark Papers." Colonel Isaac Clark Collection, Special Collections, University of Vermont Library, www.scfindingaids.uvm.edu.

63. Johnson and Fisher Family, "Rebecca Doty."

64. Ibid.

65. Colonel Seth Warner's Extra-Continental Regiment, "Biography."

66. Broom, "Ebenezer Allen."

Chapter 6

67. Broom, "Ebenezer Allen, II," 2.

68. Dixon, "Col. Ebeneezer Allen," 964, 979.

69. Hayward, *Gazetteer*, 211–16.

70. Ibid.

71. Ibid.

72. Gabriel, "Trophies and Plunder."

73. Austin, "Pension Application."

74. Mullen, personal email communication with the author, November 4, 2020.

75. Broom, "Ebenezer Allen, II," 5.

76. Hemenway, *The History of Rutland County*, 1,147.

77. Selig, "Cultural Resources Survey."

78. Gabriel, "Boutelle's Diary," 25.

79. Ibid.

80. Robinson, Rowland, *Vermont, A Study of Independence*, 177.

81. Vermont Historical Society, *Collections*, 227.

82. Hoyt, "Pawlet Expedition," 79.

83. Ibid.

84. George Washington's Mount Vernon, "Fire Cakes."

85. Zlatich, "You Asked."

86. Ibid.

87. Crockett, *Vermont*, 157.

88. Stratton, "South Hero Island," 6.
89. Crockett, *Vermont*, 157.
90. Kingsley, "German Perspective," 18–19.
91. Ibid.
92. Ibid.
93. Hoyt, "Pawlet Expedition."
94. Broom, "Ebenezer Allen, II."

Chapter 7

95. Dixon, "Col. Ebeneezer Allen," 581.
96. Ibid.; Hoyt, "Pawlet Expedition."
97. Ibid.
98. History, "Vermont Declares Independence."
99. Avalon Project, "Constitution of Vermont."
100. Ibid.
101. French, "Markers."
102. Wren, *Turbulent Sons*.
103. Kelley, "UVM Slavery Study," 1.
104. Van Buskirk, "Crossing the Lines," 78.
105. Whitfield, email communication with the author, October 19, 2020.
106. Underhill, phone and email communication with the author, October 22, 2020
107. Hance, phone communication with the author, October 22, 2020.
108. Cox, "Jacob House."
109. Sauchelli and Hanson, "Windsor Grapples."
110. Ibid.

Chapter 8

111. Dana, "New Haven."
112. Pemberton, "Justus Sherwood."
113. Ibid.; Churchill, *Hubbardton*, 3.
114. Allen, "Orders."
115. Bushnell, "Then Again."
116. Hoth, ed., "Schuyler," 654–56.
117. Barnes, *Short Biography*, 7.
118. Pemberton, "Justus Sherwood."
119. Healey, interview in person and by email with the author, July 2020.
120. Sons of the American Revolution, *Official Bulletin*.

121. Pemberton, "Haldimand Negotiations."
122. Pemberton, "Justus Sherwood."
123. Duffy, "Ethan Allen."
124. Lengel, ed., "Joseph Reed," 449.
125. Pemberton, "Justus Sherwood," 88.
126. Auburn, "West Point."
127. Founders Online, "Joseph Marsh."
128. Duffy, "Ethan Allen," 17.
129. Public Archives of Canada, "John Taplin's Information," Haldimand Papers, B.177-2, 4IO, July 31, 1782; Wren, *Turbulent Sons*, 121.

Chapter 9

130. Barnes, Short Biography, 7.
131. Dixon, "Grand Isle."
132. Strauss, "Apocalypses."
133. Marvin, "Alburgh."
134. Dixon, "Grand Isle."
135. Ibid.
136. Gauthier, "Historical Narrative."
137. Hirsch, "Colonial-Era Drinks."
138. Allen, *His Kin*, 151, 160.
139. Hall, *Eastern Vermont*, 317.
140. Allen, "Bill from Ebenezer Allen."
141. Hall, *Eastern Vermont*, 317.
142. Haviland and Power, *Original Vermonters*.
143. Thompson, *History*.
144. Barnes, Short Biography, 8.
145. Pomeroy, Esq. "Recollections."
146. Ibid.
147. Gillen, *Prince and His Lady*, 82.
148. Ibid.
149. Ibid.
150. Allen, "Letter from Ebenezer Allen."
151. Founders Online, "The Case of Robert Randall and Charles Whitney."
152. Durfee and Gregory, *Guide*, 96.
153. *Records of the Governor*, 514.

Chapter 10

154. Gellman, "Vision and Division," 36.
155. Taft, Esq., "Documents and Sketches."
156. Caselaw Access Project, "Pearl v. Allen."
157. King, "City Hall Block."
158. Taft, Esq., "Documents and Sketches." 496
159. Caselaw Access Project, "Pearl v. Allen."
160. Ibid.
161. Barnes, *Short Biography*, 13.

BIBLIOGRAPHY

Aldrich, Lewis Cass, ed. *History of Franklin and Grand Isle Counties, Vermont: With Illustrations and Biographical Sketches of Some of the Prominent Men and Pioneers.* Syracuse, NY: D. Mason and Co., 1891. www.books.google.com.

Allen, Ethan. *Ethan Allen & His Kin: Correspondence, 1772–1819.* Vols. 1 and 2. John J. Duffy, ed., with Ralph H. Orth, J. Kevin Graffagnino and Michael A. Bellesiles. Hanover, NH: University Press of New England, 1998.

———. "Orders from Thomas Chittenden, Concerning East-Side Uprisings in 'Great Cow War' (broadside, photostat)." June 7, 1779. Allen Family Papers, University of Vermont Libraries, Special Collections. www.scfindingaids.uvm.edu.

Allen, Ira. "Agreement with Ebenezer Allen, for Cutting and Shipping 150,000 Feet of White Pine Lumber to Quebec." Allen Family Papers, University of Vermont Libraries, Special Collections. November 29, 1792. scfindingaids.uvm.edu.

———. "Letter from Ebenezer Allen, Requesting Greater Assistance from Ira in Money Matters." Allen Family Papers, University of Vermont Libraries, Special Collections. January 31, 1795. www.scfindingaids.uvm.edu.

Allen, Levi. "Bill from Ebenezer Allen, for Handkerchiefs, Cloth and Shoes." Allen Family Papers, University of Vermont Libraries, Special Collections. October 10, 1788. www.scfindingaids.uvm.edu.

———. "Letter to Ira Allen, Urging Him to Keep Vermont from Joining the Union." Allen Family Papers, University of Vermont Libraries, Special Collections. August 20, 1791. www.scfindingaids.uvm.edu.

Allen, Orrin P. *The Allen Memorial: Second Series, Descendants of Samuel Allen of Windsor, Conn., 1604–1907.* Palmer, MA: C.B. Fiske & Company, 1907. www.archive.org.

American Academy of Pediatrics. "On the Treatment of Diphtheria in 1735." *Pediatrics,* January 1, 1975, www.pediatrics.aappublications.org.

BIBLIOGRAPHY

Ashley, Elias. "Poultney." *Vermont Historical Gazetteer* 2 (1877): 964–79. books.google.com.

Auburn, Emma. "West Point." George Washington's Mount Vernon, www. mountvernon.org.

AuctionZip. "Lot 268, WILLIAM BARTON ALS Revolutionary War Officer General Prescott Supports Him!" www.auctionzip.com.

Austin, John. "Pension Application, S22094, Stickney's New Hampshire Militia Regiment, Colonel Moses Nichols at Bennington." New York State Office of Parks, Recreation and Historic Preservation. www.parks.ny.gov.

Avalon Project. "Constitution of Vermont—July 4, 1786." Documents in Law, History and Diplomacy, Lillian Goldman Law Library. www.avalon.law.yale.edu.

Barnes, Melvin. *Reprint of a Short Biography of Colonel Ebenezer Allen: Known in the New Hampshire Grants as Captain or Major, AD 1777, Before and After: Also Short Biographies of Lieutenant Samuel Allen and Dr. Jacob Roebeck, in Addition Some Reminiscences of Lake Champlain*. Plattsburg, NY: J.W. Tuttle, 1852. www.books.google.com.

Bascom, Robert, and James Holden. "The Ticonderoga Expedition of 1775." *Proceedings from the New York State Historical Association* 9 (1910): 303–89. www.jstor.org.

Bennington Land Records. "Ebenezer Allen Emancipation, Book 3, Page 18." Bennington, Vermont.

Botta, Charles. *History of the United States*. Vol. 1. New Haven, CT: T. Brainard, 1834.

Broom, Joseph L. "Ebenezer Allen: Tinmouth's Forgotten Revolutionary War Hero?" *Tinmouth Channel* 2, no. 4 (Summer 2001): 3.

———. "Ebenezer Allen: Tinmouth's Forgotten Revolutionary War Hero? Part II." *Tinmouth Channel* 3, no. 1 (Fall 2001).

Bushnell, Mark. "Then Again: Defiant 'Yorkers' Brought to Heel during 1783 'Cow Wars.'" *VTDigger*, July 19, 2020. www.vtdigger.org.

Caselaw Access Project. "Pearl v. Allen, 2 Tyl. 311 (1803)." www.cite.case.law.

Caverly, A.M. *History of Pittsford, Vermont*. Rutland, VT: Tuttle, 1872.

Churchill, Amos. *History of Hubbardton*. Vol. 6. Rutland, VT: Tuttle, 1855.

"Colonel Isaac Clark Papers." Colonel Isaac Clark Collection, Special Collections, University of Vermont Library. www.scfindingaids.uvm.edu.

Colonel Seth Warner's Extra-Continental Regiment. "A Brief Biography of Col. Seth Warner." www.warnersregiment.org.

Cox, Heather. "The Stephen Jacob House." Historic Windsor Inc. www. preservationworks.org.

Crockett, Walter Hill. *Vermont: The Green Mountain State*. Vol. 2. New York: Century History Company, 1921. www.ancestraltrackers.net.

Dana, Edward S. "History of the Town of New Haven." Addison County. www. sites.rootsweb.com.

Darling, Anthony D. *Red Coat and Brown Bess*. Bloomfield, ON: Museum Restoration Service, 1970.

Deming, Leonard. *Catalogue of the Principal Officers of Vermont: As Connected with Its Political History, From 1778 to 1851, With Some Biographical Notices, &c.* Middlebury, VT: Self-published, 1851. www.babel.hathitrust.org.

Dixon, D. Webster. "Col. Ebeneezer Allen." *Vermont Historical Gazetteer* 2 (1871): www.books.google.com.

———. "History of the Town of Grand Isle." www.ancestry.com.

Duffy, John L. "How Ethan Allen and His Brothers Chased Success in the Real Estate Business." *Walloomsack Review*, n.d., www.benningtonmuseum.org.

Durfee, Eleazer D., and D. Gregory Sanford. *A Guide to the Henry Stevens, Sr. Collection at the Vermont State Archives.* N.p.: National Endowment for the Humanities, n.d. www.sos.vermont.gov.

Encyclopedia Americana. 30 vols. Albany, NY: J.B. Lyon Company, 1925, 26. www.books.google.com.

Founders Online. "The Case of Robert Randall and Charles Whitney, 28 December 1795–13 January 1796 (Editorial Note)." National Archives. www.founders.archives.gov.

———. "To George Washington from Joseph Marsh, 3 November 1780." National Archives. www.founders.archives.gov.

French, Ellie. "Markers Recognize People Enslaved by Ethan Allen's Daughter in Burlington." *VTDigger*, September 15, 2020. www.vtdigger.org.

Gabriel, Michael P. "Trophies and Plunder: After the Battle of Bennington." *Vermont History* 87, no. 2 (Summer/Fall 2019): 111–125. www.vermonthistory.org.

———. "William Boutelle's Diary of the Bennington Expedition." *Walloomsac Review*, n.d., www.benningtonmuseum.org.

Gauthier, Brennan. Email to the author. October 20, 2020.

———. "Historical Narrative." Vermont Barn Census, Preliminary Research, 2009. www.uvm.edu.

Gellman, Virginia Alison. "Vision and Division in a Frontier Community: Burlington, Vermont 1790–1810." Master's thesis, University of Vermont, 2007. www.citeseerx.ist.psu.edu.

George Washington's Mount Vernon. "How to Make Fire Cakes." www.mountvernon.org.

Gillen, Mollie. *The Prince and His Lady: The Love Story of the Duke of Kent and Madame de St. Laurent.* Halifax, NS: Formac Publishing, 2005. www.books.google.ca.

Goodrich, John E. *Rolls of the Soldiers in the Revolutionary War, 1775 to 1783.* Rutland, VT: Tuttle, 1904.

Goodwin, Neil. "The Narrative of the Captive: George Avery, 1780–1782." *Vermont History* 80, no. 2 (Summer/Fall 2012): 112–140. www.vermonthistory.org.

Graham, Rosalyn. "Siege of the Moses Peirson Block House." *Shelburne News*, October 22, 2015. www.vtcng.com.

BIBLIOGRAPHY

Hall, Benjamin H. *History of Eastern Vermont*. Appleton, NY: J. Munsell, 1858.

Hance, Dawn. Phone communication with the author. October 22, 2020.

Haviland, William A., and Marjory W. Power. *The Original Vermonters: Native Inhabitants Past and Present*. Lebanon, NH: University Press of New England, 1981.

Hayward, John. *Gazetteer of Vermont*. Boston: Tappan, Whittemore, and Mason, 1849. www.google.com/books.

Healey, Mary Jane. Interview in person and by email with the author. July 2020.

Hemenway, Abby Maria, ed. *The Vermont Historical Gazetteer: A Magazine, Embracing a History of Each Town, Civil, Ecclesiastical, Biographical and Military*. Vols. 2 and 6. Burlington, VT: Self-published, 1871.

Hirsch, Corin. "5 Colonial-Era Drinks You Should Know." Serious Eats, August 9, 2018. www.drinks.seriouseats.com.

History. "Vermont Declares Independence from Colony of New York." This Day in History. www.history.com, March 15, 2010. www.history.com.

Hoth, David R., ed. "To George Washington from Major General Philip Schuyler, 26 April 1778." In *The Papers of George Washington, March 1, 1778–April 30, 1778*. Revolutionary War Series. Vol. 14. Charlottesville: University of Virginia Press, 2004. 654–56. www.founders.archives.gov.

Hoyt, Edward A. "The Pawlet Expedition, September, 1777." *Vermont History* 75, no. 2 (Summer/Fall 2007): 69–100. www.vermonthistory.org.

Johnson and Fisher Family. "Rebecca Doty." www.johnsonfamily.talldude.net.

Kalif, Will. "Blacksmithing." www.stormthecastle.com.

Kelley, Kevin J. "UVM Slavery Study Challenges Vermont's Abolitionist Rep." *Seven Days*, January 15, 2014. www.sevendaysvt.com.

King, Adam. "The City Hall Block—College Street to Main Street, West Side." Historic Church Street Blocks. www.uvm.edu.

Kingsley, Ronald F. "A German Perspective on the American Attempt to Recapture the British Forts at Ticonderoga and Mount Independence on September 18, 1777." *Vermont History* 67, nos. 1 and 2 (Winter/Spring 1999): 5–26. www.vermonthistory.org.

Lengel, Edward G., ed. "From George Washington to Joseph Reed, November 25, 1775." In *The Papers of George Washington*. Charlottesville: University of Virginia Press, 2008, 449. www.rotunda.upress.virginia.edu.

MacGuire, J. Robert. "The British Secret Service and the Attempt to Kidnap Jacob Bayley." *Vermont History* 44, no. 3 (Summer 1976): 141–67. www.vermonthistory.org.

Marvin, David. "History of the Town of Alburgh." www.ancestry.com.

Minkema, Kenneth P. "Jonathan Edwards's Defense of Slavery." *Massachusetts Historical Review (Race & Slavery)* 4 (2002): 23–59. www.edwardseducationblog.files.wordpress.com.

Morabito, Margaret. "Way Back When: Tithing Men." First Congregational Church, United Church of Christ, 2015, www.rindgechurch.org.

BIBLIOGRAPHY

Mullen, Jerry. Personal phone and email communication with the author. November 4, 2020.

Nye, Mary Greene. "Loyalists and Their Property." *Proceedings of the Vermont Historical Society* 10, no. 1 (March 1942): 36–44. www.vermonthistory.org.

Order of the Legislature. *A Journal of the General Assembly of the State of Vermont. Oct. 1800.* Bennington, VT: Anthony Haswell, 1801. www.babel.hathitrust.org.

Paxton, James. *Joseph Brant and His World: 18th Century Mohawk Warrior and Statesmen.* Toronto, ON: James Lormier & Company, 2008.

Pemberton, Ian Cleghorn. "The British Secret Service in the Champlain Valley During the Haldimand Negotiations, 1780–1783." *Vermont History* 44, no. 3 (Summer 1976): 129–40. www.vermonthistory.org.

———. "Justus Sherwood, Vermont Loyalist, 1747–1798." PhD diss., University of Western Ontario, 1973. www.ir.lib.uwo.ca.

Philbrick, Nathaniel. *Bunker Hill: A City, a Siege, a Revolution.* New York: Penguin, 2013.

Pomeroy, J.N., Esq. "From Recollections of Horace Loomis." *Vermont Historical Magazine,* n.d. www.sites.rootsweb.com.

Poultney Historical Society. "Colonial Times to Independence (1761–1777)." www.poultneyhistoricalsociety.org.

Powers, Bill. "Ebenezer Allen Bio." Unpublished manuscript, 2020.

———. Phone interview with the author. October 27, 2020.

Procknow, Gene. "The Rebel and the Tory: Ethan Allen, Philip Skene, and the Dawn of Vermont." *Journal of the American Revolution,* May 11, 2020. www.allthingsliberty.com.

Public Archives of Canada. "John Taplin's Information." Haldimand Papers, B.177-2, 4IO. July 31, 1782.

Records of the Governor and Council of the State of Vermont. Vol. 3. Montpelier, VT: E.P. Walton, 1875. www.books.google.com.

Reynolds, Grant. Email to author. October 16, 2020.

Richmond, Vermont. "History, Richmond, Vermont: A Town Through Time." www.richmondvt.gov.

Robinson, Douglas. "Col Timothy Allen (1765–1832)." Find a Grave. www.findagrave.com.

Robinson, Rowland. *Vermont, A Study of Independence.* New York: Houghton Mifflin, 1892.

Sauchelli, Lisa, and Alex Hanson. "Windsor Grapples with Evidence That a Major Figure in Town, Vermont History Was a Slaveholding Scofflaw." *Valley News,* July 25, 2020. www.vnews.com.

Selig, Robert. "Cultural Resources Survey of the Bennington Battlefield Walloomsac, New York." New York State Office of Parks, Recreation, and Historic Preservation, October 2017. www.parks.ny.gov.

Smith, Donald A. "Green Mountain Insurgency: Transformation of New York's Forty Year Land War." *Vermont History* 64, no. 4 (Fall 1996): 197–217. www.vermonthistory.org.

Smith, H.P., and W.S. Rann, eds. *History of Rutland County, Vermont: With Illustrations and Biographical Sketches of Some of Its Prominent Men and Pioneers.* Facsimile reprint, Bowie, MD: Heritage Books, 1993. www.books.google.com.

Sons of the American Revolution. *Official Bulletin of the National Society of the Sons of the American Revolution* 9, no. 2 (October 1914). www.sar.org.

Spencer, Mark G., ed. "Allen, Ethan (1738–89)." In *The Bloomsbury Encyclopedia of the American Enlightenment.* New York: Bloomsbury, 2015. www.books.google.com.

Stratton, Allen L. "History of the South Hero Island: Being the Towns of South Hero and Grand Isle, Vermont." *Rutland Weekly Herald,* July 30, 1868, 6.

Strauss, Mark. "Ten Notable Apocalypses That (Obviously) Didn't Happen." *Smithsonian Magazine,* November 12, 2009. www.smithsonianmag.com.

Taft, Russell S., Esq. "Documents and Sketches Relating to the Early History of Burlington, Vermont." www.ancestry.com.

Thompson, Zadock. *History of the State of Vermont: From Its Earliest Settlement to the Close of the Year 1832.* Burlington, VT: Edward Smith, 1833. www.books.google.com.

Tice, Joyce M. "Epidemics and Pandemics in the U.S.: 1616–Present." History Center on Main Street, November 21, 2004. www.joycetice.com.

Underhill, Bob. Phone and email communication with the author. October 22, 2020.

Underwood, Wynn. "Indian and Tory Raids on the Otter Valley 1777–1782." *Vermont History Journal* 15, no. 4 (October 1947): 195–221. www.vermonthistory.org.

United States Army. *Ranger Handbook.* Fort Benning, GA: United States Army Infantry School, 2000. www.shu.edu.

Van Buskirk, Judith. "Crossing the Lines: African-Americans in the New York City Region During the British Occupation, 1776–1783." *Pennsylvania History* 65 (1998): 74–100. www.jstor.org.

Vermont Historical Society. *Collections of the Vermont Historical Society.* Montpelier, VT: J. and J.M. Poland, 1870. www.brittlebooks.library.illinois.edu.

VTD editor. "In This State: Historian Finds Imprecise End to Slavery in Vermont." *VTDigger,* February 23, 2014. www.vtdigger.org.

Walton, E.P. *State of Vermont.* Vol. 4. Montpelier, VT: J. & J.M. Poland, 1876. www.babel.hathitrust.org.

Whitfield, Harvey A. Email communication with the author. October 19, 2020.

Wren, Christopher S. *Those Turbulent Sons of Freedom: Ethan Allen's Green Mountain Boys and the American Revolution.* New York: Simon & Schuster, 2019.

Zlatich, Marko. "You Asked, We Answered: What Did Soldiers Eat during the Revolutionary War?" National Museum of American History, January 21, 2015. www.americanhistory.si.edu.

INDEX

Index

ABOUT THE AUTHOR

Glenn Fay's New England roots precede the American Revolution, and he was born in Middlebury, Vermont. As a kid, he was naturally drawn to Vermont's woods, lakes and streams, where he spent time with his family, especially his grandfather. Glenn has lived in or spent time in Windsor, Addison, Rutland, Orleans, Grand Isle and Chittenden Counties. He helped raise two kids in South Hero; he taught middle and high school students, and he worked as an adjunct professor for years at the University of Vermont.

In 1993, Glenn was awarded an NSF-funded fellowship to study the environmental impacts of the maritime War of 1812 in the Champlain Valley. During this experience, the remarkable and dramatic history of Vermont and its ghosts of the past came to life. That experience planted seeds of interest and began the research that would lead to a deep interest in preserving Vermont's past so its residents might hear its echoes and learn from them.

When he is not engaged in researching the past or writing, Glenn can be found trekking and exploring old haunts in the Champlain Islands, on Lake Champlain, in the Green Mountains and beyond.

Visit us at
www.historypress.com
....

Printed in the USA
CPSIA information can be obtained
at www.ICGtesting.com
LVHW051240261023
761548LV00010B/51

9 781540 247636